TRINITY CHURCH
tales to remember

TRINITY CHURCH

tales to remember

Meg Grimm

Copyright 2020 by the author Meg Grimm

All rights reserved. This book or any portion thereof may not be reproduced or used in any manner whatsoever without the express written permission of the publisher except for the use of brief quotations in a book review or scholarly journal.

Story Spinner Press
Ohiopyle, Pennsylvania

www.storyspinnerbooks.com

All Scripture quotations, unless otherwise indicated, are taken from THE HOLY BIBLE, NEW INTERNATIONAL VERSION®, NIV® Copyright © 1973, 1978, 1984, 2011 by Biblica, Inc.® Used by permission. All rights reserved worldwide.

The website addresses and print books recommended throughout this book are offered as resources and do not in any way imply an endorsement on the part of Story Spinner Press, LLC.

Second Edition, December 2020

Printed in the United States of America

ISBN 978-1-7347867-3-6

Library of Congress Control Number: 2020924374

TRINITY CHURCH

tales to remember

Meg Grimm

Copyright 2020 by the author Meg Grimm

All rights reserved. This book or any portion thereof may not be reproduced or used in any manner whatsoever without the express written permission of the publisher except for the use of brief quotations in a book review or scholarly journal.

Story Spinner Press
Ohiopyle, Pennsylvania

www.storyspinnerbooks.com

All Scripture quotations, unless otherwise indicated, are taken from THE HOLY BIBLE, NEW INTERNATIONAL VERSION®, NIV® Copyright © 1973, 1978, 1984, 2011 by Biblica, Inc.® Used by permission. All rights reserved worldwide.

The website addresses and print books recommended throughout this book are offered as resources and do not in any way imply an endorsement on the part of Story Spinner Press, LLC.

Second Edition, December 2020

Printed in the United States of America

ISBN 978-1-7347867-3-6

Library of Congress Control Number: 2020924374

Dedicated to faithful members of Trinity Church – past, present and future

preface to the second edition

I WILL ALWAYS BE GRATEFUL FOR THE PARISHIONERS OF TRINITY CHURCH FOR HAVING ALLOWED ME THE PRIVILEGE TO WRITE ABOUT THEM, and for their support of my first book.

Trinity Church Tales to Remember really was my first independently published book, but I had a different last name then, and no LLC. I only had my love for history and for Trinity Church.

I had wanted to contribute to the efforts of many others through the years to preserve the story of this special church. My vision for the book was always a collection of tales to be told in the whimsical voice of folklore, so that the stories might catch the attention of a wider audience. To me, telling history in the form of narrative is really the only way to tell it if you want it to be remembered. And I did.

It was nothing short of a miracle that the book was available in time for Christmas 2015. The production process was new to me, and I had not anticipated all that it would entail. At the time, I was working with a young, computer-savvy photographer, who was very patient with my shortcomings. If it had not been for him, the book would never have made it into the parishioner's hands by that holiday season. Two years later, I married the photographer, and he has been helping me produce books ever since.

I decided to make a second edition to this book because I have learned a lot since that time. I wanted to give it my best again, because those at Trinity Church have always deserved my best.

Please enjoy this delightful journey into the glory days of an area rich in history, from eighteenth century pioneers to glamorous playhouses, from prohibition to present day. May it awaken something inside of you that you might not have known was there.

Meg Grimm

OHIOPYLE- PA.-
fall 2020

table of contents

a most unusual incident   **1**

the watchmen and their star-crossed temples   **6**

dawning of the bitter root   **16**

the case of the tiffany windows   **28**

the house of the promise children   **35**

j. v. thompson and the theory of the myth   **47**

the heirs of castle stirling   **56**

the name in lights   **68**

the mystery of the silent tower   **80**

a trinity house ghost story   **86**

that they all may be one   **95**

the road from port charlotte   **107**

a narrow escape   **123**

chronicle of a legacy   **128**

Uniontown 1872

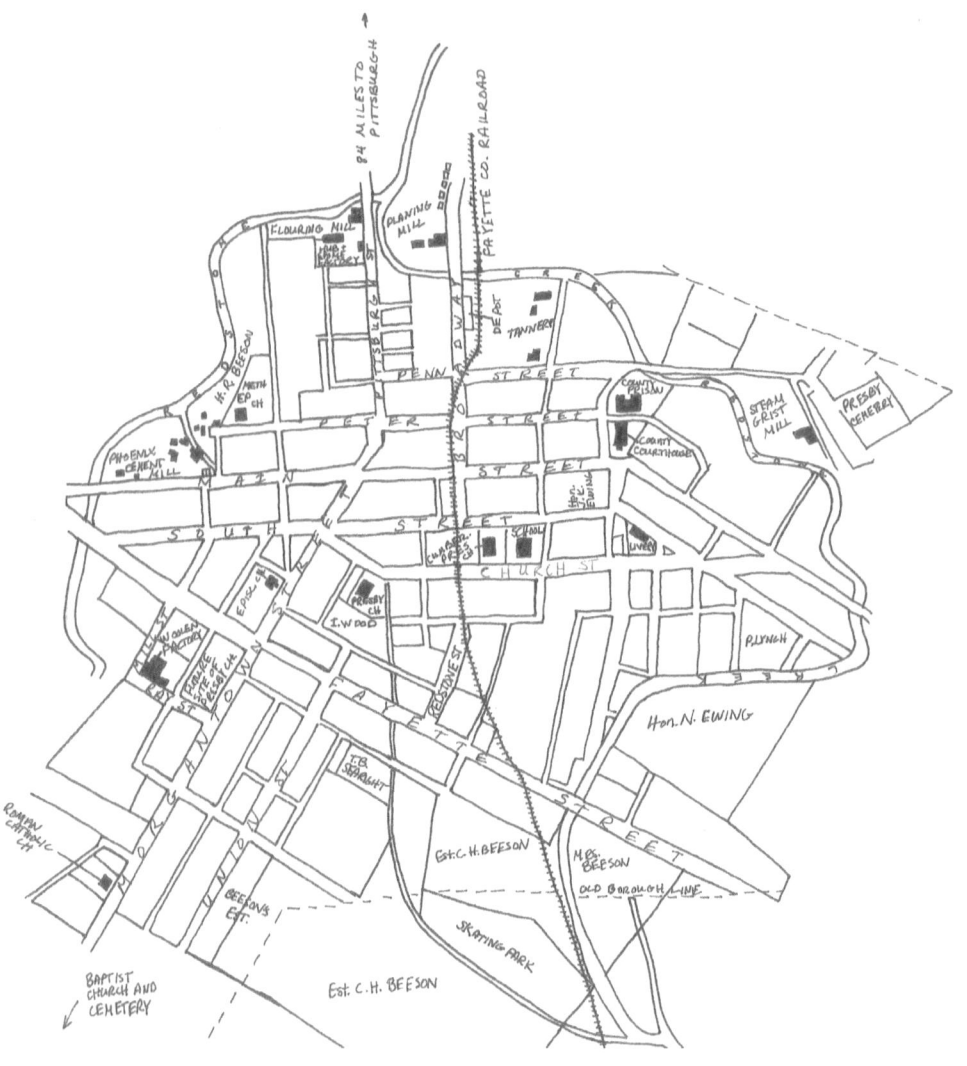

a most unusual incident

IN THE YEAR 1939, Americans were carrying on with business as usual but keeping a careful eye on the trouble overseas. The United States had proclaimed neutrality and hoped for the best. Little did they know the nation would be involved in the Second World War within the next two years following the devastating bombing of their Pearl Harbor. In the meantime, the Great Depression had finally lost its firm grip on the country.

In Uniontown, Pennsylvania, Miss Ethel Boughner least expected to play a large role in uncovering the key to the oldest mystery of the First Presbyterian Church, but that is exactly what happened.

As a member of the congregation since March 1905 and a local historian, Miss Boughner may have often been asked about pioneer families from the area. Then as now, people were interested in learning about their ancestors who had gone before them. On a crisp autumn day, Miss Boughner received one such inquiry.

A woman had come to Uniontown from Massillon, Ohio to visit the Uniontown courthouse and substantiate some facts she had gleaned from her family's written records. The woman was a descendent of Robert Moore, Esq., a previous resident of Wharton Township. Her ancestors were all of Revolutionary War stock and had moved to Ohio in 1804. To the woman's delight, Miss Boughner was able to provide some extra assistance.

Not long after the woman had gone back home, Miss Boughner was contacted again. The woman's family needed some "additional details." It seemed the Moores had in their possession an old diary once kept by Robert. As various names were rattled off from the pages to Miss Boughner, her eyes lit up. She excitedly informed the family that those people had not only been pioneers from Uniontown, but they were involved with founding the First Presbyterian Church.

From then on, the Moores kept in touch with Miss Boughner frequently to compare notes. Eventually, something else unexpected happened.

The family had long known about an old trunk that once belonged to Robert, but they did not know it had any significance to the church back in Uniontown. Upon inspection, and with Miss Boughner's historical knowledge, it was discovered that this special box contained documents telling of the organization of the congregation in 1799. It seemed that when the Moore pioneers had left Uniontown with their belongings tied to pack horses and mules, the priceless contents in the trunk had bobbed along with them.

As of 1876, Dr. Hugh Campbell, an elder and pillar of the church, once delivered a sermon to the First Presbyterian congregation in which he stated that they did not have the original church records. Then, in 1888, the year when a second written history of the congregation was compiled, still no record had been found with the date of the church's organization. When the new church building was erected in 1896, the Reverend Dr. Alexander Milholland reiterated the same.

By 1939, the congregation had long abandoned hope of discovering the old record. Miss Boughner could not have been more surprised. She coordinated with the Moores to have the records turned over to the Reverend Dr. William Blake Hindman. It was October and just days away from the 140th anniversary of the organization of the church, as it turned out.

According to the recovered documents, an original supplication made to the Redstone Presbytery had been acted upon on October 12, 1799 when the original small group of Presbyterians requested pastoral supplies with which to establish their congregation. They made consistent mention of their fragile state as they referred to themselves as an "infant congregation" in a "desolate condition."

At their meeting on September 30, they had written to Presbytery the following:

> *In full assurance that this our prayer will be heard and that God in His mercy will enable you to take such a fostering care of these our infant struggles as will be most for the increase of righteousness advantage of immortal souls and interest in the glorious cause of the Gospel.*

The records of Redstone Presbytery tell their response:

At the meeting at Georges Creek, October 12, application was made for supplies by the vacant congregation at Uniontown, and the Rev. James Power was appointed for one Sabbath and Rev. Samuel Porter for another.

The presbytery itself had only just become constituted as of May 1781. The area it served was known as the Great West. It was "bounded on the east by the Allegheny Mountains, on the north by Lake Erie, on the south by Virginia, and on the west by the setting sun." The Town of Union, as Henry Beeson had named it, being embedded in the middle of this, was included.

The Reverend James Power became the first ordained Presbyterian minister to settle with his family in western Pennsylvania. Other early ministers to the area were the Reverends Joseph Smith and John McMillan. These men were described as pious, patient, and laborious. They did for their people all that their circumstances would allow, and that was not much.

In those days, ministers courageously braved the dangers of carrying the Gospel to scattered settlements in the area and also to the natives. The rough peoples they met eventually began to receive them courteously.

Many of Uniontown's early and yet unestablished congregations held their Sabbath services in the dense woods with logs to sit upon and log pulpits, or sometimes pulpits constructed of a few rough slabs covered with clapboards. Even in cold weather, God-fearing, sturdy folk gathered and listened to sermons that were often 1 ½ hours long, and two of them each Sabbath.

It was coming up out of these days of shady groves and tents for church buildings that the Presbyterian group of believers had requested supplies. Firmly establishing a church congregation was difficult for any settlers. They suffered from native attacks, lack of houses for worship, and even lack of food and clothing.

On July 24, 1800, the committee that had been appointed to superintend the business of the Presbyterian congregation, through Robert Moore, acknowledged the response of the Presbytery with thanks. They wrote that they hoped the Presbytery would favor their endeavors for the propagation of the Gospel, trusting that "through Divine assistance a Church may be organized" in the region. The founders of the church then proceeded to lay the groundwork for the financial undertakings of the new organization.

How proud they must have been to formally make a place for themselves in the religious life of their community. They had already emerged through difficulties and discouragements, hard labor and heartaches. Now the joy of success was theirs.

The first church meetings of the newly established congregation were held in the local courthouse and then later in the home of Jake Beeson. A real church building to call their own was not erected for 28 years after their establishment. Nevertheless, during that time, the "infant congregation" grew and flourished. Their institution had not been started by ministers or by the Presbytery, but by people living in early Uniontown who sought to be nurtured in the faith and to see the Gospel of Jesus Christ spread in their domain. Their ambitions were marked with humility and unity.

Over two centuries later, the congregation has stood the test of time. The labors of their predecessors prevailed, and the Document of Organization was a testament of that labor.

Not many churches formed in the 1700s still possess their original records. Given the conditions of the time, that is not hard to believe. Yet our Sovereign God saw fit to resurface the 140-years-lost article of the Presbyterian Church of Uniontown on one quiet day in 1939, just before another great war would rock the United States and change the priorities of most people. The document may never have been found at all. Instead, it surfaced just in time for the church to celebrate with pride and certainty their 140th anniversary.

What do you think? Coincidence?

Sources

Newspaper:

"Official Foundation Document of First Presbyterian Church Found." *The Morning Herald* 13 Oct. 1939: 1, 10. *http://www.newspapers.com*. Web. 11 Nov. 2015

Website:

"World War II in Europe." *The History Place.* The History Place, n.d. Web. 6 June 2015. <http://www.historyplace.com/worldwar2/timeline/ ww2time. htm>

Church Records:

The Second Presbyterian Church Uniontown, Pennsylvania, Fiftieth Anniversary. Uniontown, 1943. Print. (Church Booklet)

A Brief History of the First Presbyterian Church of Uniontown, Pa.: As pertaining more especially to the Erection and Dedication of The Building which was set apart to the service of God March 8, 1896. Uniontown; Genius of Liberty, n.d. Print. (Church Booklet)

Hindman, William B. *Brief History of the First Presbyterian Church of Uniontown Pa.* Uniontown, n.d. Print. (Notes left behind by the Rev. Dr. William Blake Hindman)

Note: The original Document of Organization was later lost again. In a three-page typed *Brief History of the First Presbyterian Church Uniontown Pa* that appears to have been authored by the Rev. Dr. William Blake Hindman (Pastorate: 1928-1953), he writes the following: "The paper was borrowed from me by a member of the Session to make photocopies. It was never returned. Said to be lost. Few churches have such a paper. I am sorry it is missing." As far as is known, the document has not resurfaced.

the watchmen and their star-crossed temples

Watchman, tell us of the night, what its signs of promise are.
Traveler, what a wondrous sight: see that glory-beaming star.
Watchman, does its beauteous ray news of joy or hope foretell?
Traveler, yes; it brings the day, promised day of Israel.

from Watchman, Tell Us of The Night, a Christmas hymn by John Bowring, 1825

WHEREVER THERE HAS BEEN THE PROPAGATION OF THE GOSPEL, the devil has been known to try and thwart the attempts. Especially in the darkest hour of a Christian's life, the tempter's method is to keep the saint's mind on their present miseries and discouragement. One of two results can be expected. Either the saint succumbs to the hopelessness of despair, or they, like Saint James implores us, "count it all joy," knowing that the trying of faith worketh patience.

The nineteenth century was an exciting time for the First Presbyterian Church congregation. Their growth had been slow, but it was steady. In 1825, the membership was 53 persons of whom 42 were women. This rose to 157 by 1843 and 310 by 1888. Around every corner came new advancements in their realm, and each shepherd of the flock was just as adored as the last. In those days, the pastor of a church was considered a leader in the community. His opinions carried great weight. This was particularly true in the Presbyterian Church.

However, not unlike most others in those days, the young congregation was forced to endure the battering of many large-scale trials and tragedies. One such problem they in particular seemed to inevitably face throughout the century was that they never could quite keep a building. Each one was always eventually stripped from them one way or another.

First Presbyterian Church
1820

Construction of their very first humble home was started near the southwest corner of Morgantown and South Streets in the year 1824. It was likely accompanied by the usual toil and worry of a large project. The erection of the structure took three years to complete. It was finished in January, and the total cost was around $3,000. The congregation was probably ecstatic to have a home of their own after many long years of meeting in the courthouse. But their celebrations would soon be stamped out when objections began.

As it turned out, the structure had been built on public ground that was donated by Jacob Beeson and designated to the town as a market place or other public uses. The plain, one-story brick house that contained old-fashioned high

Second Church Building 1838
Church St.

back pews and an elevated pulpit was only allowed to stand for about 10 years. Agitating opposition ran the poor fledgling congregation right out the doors. Records show that a town resident was even prosecuted and held under bond for tearing down a fence that had surrounded the church meeting house.

Wanting to help, a Mr. Isaac Wood purchased the lot upon which the next building would stand. The second meeting house went up between 1837 and 1838, and it stood back a little from the road along Church Street. The architect and builder, William Redick, had put extra special care into the project. After all, he was a church member and an elder on the church session.

The new house was completed in the springtime. A golden sun shone upon it while blossoms perhaps permeated the air. This structure was made of brick and had a vestibule, steeple, and bell. Inside, it may have smelled of fresh plaster and hope. Light, it seemed, from heaven itself poured into the wide, open space from the soaring windows, which were tall enough to accommodate the building's two stories. This house was considerably larger and more pretentious than the first, and the total cost came to about $5,500.

To the grateful church members, it was probably the most glorious and imposing new building in all of Uniontown. Yet in time, some felt that it ought to have been even more "satisfactory." Nevertheless, the Presbyterians managed to hold onto the second house for ten years longer than the other, but with the springtime of 1857, the reign of fortune ended.

One fateful day, a fire originating from a stove pipe burst to life. It raced through the interior of the beautiful sanctuary like a ravenous monster gobbling prey. Orange flames licked the walls hungrily, refusing to die. When the smoke finally cleared, the church members picked up their sunken hearts from the smoldering debris and walked around to assess the damage. It was determined that the faithful should tear down what remained and erect their third edifice.

Although considerably shaken, but undaunted by the misfortune, construction began at once. The congregation was apparently aglow with spiritual wellness, and they were financially stable to welcome an opportunity for an updated structure. Besides, some of the material for the new house could still be taken from the damaged one.

This second victory must have so angered that enemy of their souls, who would have rather seen them crumble than to put on happy faces and find the good.

The new, semi-gothic, third building went up with a pleasant spirit. It was a 47-by-75-foot structure, also brick, and it had two stories with a belfry and spire. In line with the times, it was lighted by gas. Another new feature that thrilled the determined congregation was their new stained-glass windows.

The total cost for the third house came to about $10,000, which was affordable for the time. The congregation was said to have had good management and were building in a favorable year.

Over the course of the following 35 years, any fears of fire gradually left the hearts of those who remembered it, fading somewhat into the ashes of the distant past.

Third Church Building 1860, Church St.

In the year 1893, the Central Presbyterian Church (later to be called Second Presbyterian) was organized, decreasing the attendance at First Church. Even with this, the need for more seating capacity at First Church had been felt for some time. Thus, the plans to erect a fourth and more commodious house commenced.

The next and most grievous event would not affect those who had remained faithful to First Church, though they only narrowly escaped. Instead, the newly established Second Church would receive its first major blow in the most unfortunate way yet.

The Watchmen and Their Star-Crossed Temples

Central Church needed a building. First Church so happened to have one, but they had sold the edifice to a Professor Griffith for $14,000 to be used as an academy. He in turn decided to sell it in September 1883 for the same sum to a Mr. Edgar J. Frost of the Central Church. (Edgar J. Frost is a fictitious name.) Mr. Frost was of the party responsible for the Presbyterian Church split, and he spent much of his fortune to secure the meeting house for the "real" Presbyterian church of Uniontown, according to him. Mr. Frost claimed that First Church was only Presbyterian in name and not in action. The full story of Mr. Frost and the Central Presbyterian Church occupies another place in this volume.

However, First Church continued to use the building for their Sabbath services and held full possession of it through a year-long lease agreement following its sale. In the meantime, plans were being drawn and preparations started for their new, fourth building. The long-time First Church members were just as happy to meet for a while longer in the third edifice, as they were reverently attached to it.

When First Church finally moved out at the end of their lease, Central Church immediately began any necessary repairs to the third building. They worked endlessly and joyfully for two months, anticipating the wonderful day when they would hold their first meeting there. They also repaired parts of the Grand Opera House, where they were meeting in the meantime.

On the night of Monday, November 12, 1894, tragedy struck. The building, now nearly ready again for occupancy, was totally destroyed by the second blazing fire on that lot in church history.

First Church had been spared this devastation by mere months. Central Church members watched in shock as their dreams fell to the scorched ground. They had not yet moved in, but their hopes and finances were so deeply threaded into the walls that it was as if life's carpet had been pulled out from under them.

Mr. Frost writes:

> This almost burned the life out of the church, but I determined I would not give up and on the next Sabbath after the fire, Dr. Gordon preached a memorable sermon in which he told us plainly that it was all for our good and that the Lord would provide us a new home if we only trusted in Him and labored earnestly. This helped our people much and soon we were at work trying to build a new home.

Indeed, a Central Church congregational meeting was held the next day after the fire to lay plans for rebuilding. The new structure began to rise right away from the ashes of the old and was mostly completed by 1895. At that time, the congregation met in the Sabbath School room until the sanctuary was officially opened. The building was declared finished on January 6, 1901.

It is important to note here that, miraculously, neither the records of the First nor the Central Presbyterian Churches of Uniontown were lost during any transition or blaze.

It follows that at the turn of the century, two new, beautiful and comfortable Presbyterian places of worship graced the skyline of Uniontown. As the congregations bid goodbye to the 1800s, they welcomed the new century with a feeling of renewed promise. Both First and Central Church had risen from the rubble of their past, and now their new stone fortress homes offered a sense of safety and security. It perhaps seemed as though the misfortune that had always plagued their beloved structures just might be behind them.

On the dedication Sunday for the fourth First Church edifice on the corner of Morgantown and Fayette Streets, Dr. D. C. Marquis of Chicago, classmate of the current pastor Dr. A. S. Milholland from McCormick Theological Seminary, preached the finale to the day's impressive proceedings at the evening service. The sanctuary was crowded almost to overflowing in the brilliant illumination of the electric and gas lights.

"Watchman, what of the night?" Dr. Marquis asked in a strong, reverberating voice. We can imagine that all eyes were fixed upon him.

This had been the question shouted up to the watchman of Isaiah 21:11-12. It was, Dr. Marquis said, the question of an enemy. Confident of victory, the enemy stood just outside the silent, sad walls of a beleaguered city.

The questioner, Dr. Marquis said, was actually taunting the watchman by pointing out his wretched condition. But the watchman stared beyond the gloom by which he was surrounded and the distress of the city, and looked to the future.

"The morning cometh," he replied.

Likewise, in the blackest night of the Church of Jesus Christ, the unbeliever still hurls the taunting question, "What of the night?" This is that trick of the crafty adversary. He does not want the struggling saints to look to the future. For they, like the watchman, may see the blush of the coming day and reply, "The morning cometh."

The lives of the Presbyterian Church congregations of Uniontown were not always bright and could not always be. Though just as the sun rises each morning, the dark nights end as well. The Christian, said Dr. Marquis, must stand not only on the mountain tops of hope but also sometimes in the shadowy valleys of doubt and despair. Then the tempter will ask, as he must have asked the members of First and Second Churches with every fiery trial of the nineteenth century, "What of the night?" At such hours, Christians must in faith, like the watchman and like those undaunted brothers and sisters before us, point to the coming morning.

Sources

Newspaper:

"The Temple Dedicated." *The News Standard* [Uniontown] 9 Mar. 1896: 1. Print.

Church Records:

The Second Presbyterian Church Uniontown, Pennsylvania, Fiftieth Anniversary. Uniontown, 1943. Print. (Church Booklet)

A Brief History of the First Presbyterian Church of Uniontown, Pa.: As pertaining more especially to the Erection and Dedication of The Building which was set apart to the service of God March 8, 1896. Uniontown; Genius of Liberty, n.d. Print. (Church Booklet)

Handwritten document by E. J. Frost (Fictitious Name)

The Watchmen and Their Star-Crossed Temples

Site of the session room after the fire, 1895

dawning of the bitter root

Looking diligently lest any man fail of the grace of God;
lest any root of bitterness springing up trouble you, and thereby many be defiled...

Hebrews 12:15 (KJV)

We would like to believe that an offshoot of First Presbyterian Church became Second Presbyterian Church solely in the spirit of growing and spreading Presbyterianism through the area at the turn of the twentieth century. Instead, history tells a different tale. In this somber account, it appears that the human heart may be entirely responsible for negative events leading to the crucial division. This should come as no surprise since Saint Matthew clearly warns about the evil lurking within the chambers of this very spiritual organ.

Our two-part tale begins over one hundred years before this writing. The author does not claim to have ever met or spoken with descendants of the parties involved but has only made speculation with respect for landing as close to the truth as possible. The facts remain, but a person's character can only be surmised.

This tale falls into a category of stories that are impossible to totally verify. That does not make them any less worthy of our telling them. For our purposes, the names of the main family involved will be changed throughout this volume. Using the detailed, lengthy and emotional accounts which those who were involved have left behind, this writer's imagination paints the story for you this way...

1 | the story of the second church

There once was a man who, as some might have said, always sat listening very attentively in his First Presbyterian Church pew with his eyes darting to and fro as to never miss the latest gossip. He seemed to hear and scrutinize every word of the sermons; and at the same time, he observed the personal lives of all those around him. If you wanted to know about your neighbor's sins, you could probably inquire of him. He was a man of great convictions of which he felt deeply and had no qualms about sharing. Records bearing his own hand seem to show that he was quick to point a finger or voice his opinions even if you did not ask.

His name for our purposes was Mr. Edgar J. Frost. He and his wife "Hannah" were somewhat new to the area. Edgar had arrived in a cold 1883 winter and secured a humble, pretty dwelling on Berkley Street. His wife had followed in April that year. Edgar made an honest, acceptable living in the hardware business.

Over the years, the couple would gradually come into the possession of a total of five children. We will call them James, Laura, Josephine, Ella and little Thomas. Eventually, the Frost family moved to 216 West Main Street in Uniontown.

Shortly after his arrival, Edgar Frost had perceived that the Presbyterian Church of Uniontown was "only one in name." Sufficient as his own income may have been, he seemed to rather dislike those who brought in significantly more than he. He associated their wealth with immoral behaviors and attitudes. These were the days before the income tax, and some of Uniontown's millionaires had risen into their fortunes. Many prestigious members of wealthy society boasted of their First Church membership.

It was at this time that we can suppose a seed of bitterness began to sprout in Edgar Frost's heart. We can imagine it taking root with minuscule claws sticking fast to the soft tissue. At this early stage, the fellow could have torn it out roots and all. Instead, it seems he decided to water it. This choice would change the Presbyterian congregation for the next fifty years. Traces of its effects are still remembered today.

Edgar, who seemed to feel quite insecure in his position at the "rich" church among the well-to-do, and who deemed himself overlooked, began to notice he was not the only one. In his opinion, the minister, the Rev. Dr. Alexander S.

Milholland, was a person who cared little for the welfare of the church so far as the young people were concerned.

"He looks not after them and only calls upon the sick. He allows his people to do as they please and says nothing, yet he knows of gross immorality," Edgar accused the Reverend, probably at first only to Hannah, who as far as can be thought had come to the same conclusions as her husband, though more delicately.

Today, we know that Dr. Milholland was praised for his strong leadership, especially when the congregation undertook the erection of their greatest church home yet. Though money does have a way of purchasing what it wants even if that is a license to sin. We may never know if Edgar's accusations were true.

Emboldened by his convictions, Edgar soon began to share these sentiments with others, some of whom were dedicated men in the church and community. To resolve the deficit of spiritual growth among the younger crowd, these folks began to lead a young men's prayer meeting. A year later, it developed into an organized young people's society. The young tend to flourish, and these did as well. They became some of the most well-respected, up and coming members of the Uniontown community.

However, this was still not enough to appease Edgar. By this time, perhaps, the bitter, little seed in his heart had become a thorny vine, wrapped and intertwined ruthlessly about the organ. He was convinced that the other churches in town were growing, but the Presbyterians were "dead."

"Presbyterianism was on the decline," he wrote later. "Hence I determined to see if I could not organize a new church."

On April 14, 1893, a number of members in agreement with Edgar met in his home to discuss the idea. They appointed a committee to attend the next meeting of Redstone Presbytery and ask them to ascertain the need and expediency of dividing the congregation in Uniontown to establish a new Presbyterian church. The petition was signed by E. J. Frost and twelve others.

Edgar declined to attend the Presbytery meeting as a commissioner but decided he could do more good to go as a regular individual on the floor. He would "thus direct the line of battle." In all this, he writes, "I was successful."

The presbytery sent a committee to survey the situation in Uniontown. The committee did recommend that a new church be established. A rather prolonged, fierce debate ensued, but the recommendation was finally adopted.

On September 14, 1893, a Thursday at 7:30 p.m., a Presbytery commission met the small group of petitioners in Commercial Hall in Uniontown. There they organized the new church and gave it the name of "The Central Presbyterian Church of Uniontown, Pennsylvania." There were 50 charter members, 48 from First Church and two from other churches. The first worship service was held at the same location the following Sabbath. Various ministers occupied the pulpit throughout the fall while the congregation prepared to call a pastor.

It would seem Edgar's determination had finally come to the end he had so long desired, but the work was only just beginning. His sacrifices, it would seem, would only feed the bitterness inside of him.

In those days, the coal industry sent a building boom sweeping through the city. Church membership nationwide rapidly increased. It was an era that became known as the Victorian age, named for Queen Victoria who reigned as the British monarch, and it was a splendid time indeed. Though not so much for the Frost family.

The first blow to the new congregation came with the fire in November 1894. Edgar had purchased the former First Church building on Church Street for the sum of $14,000, and had sold it for the same amount to Central Presbyterian. The church members worked hard to repair the building to their standards for a fresh start, but it was suddenly razed by the fire before they had even used it once.

By then, Edgar Frost and others had worked to secure the first pastor of the church, the Rev. Dr. Seth R. Gordon, who preached a memorable sermon on the Sabbath after the fire. He told the heartbroken, homeless little group that the Lord would provide. They set to work on the new building immediately, no matter that they were now severely in debt and floundering.

Edgar himself boasts of never succumbing to despair. He writes:

Through all these ♦ark an♦ trying times I have never ♦oubte♦ but all woul♦ en♦ well.

Meanwhile, little Thomas Frost had been born during the turmoil of the new church founding. He was likely toddling around with the rest of the Frost gaggle. Mrs. Hannah Frost showed her great strength in those years and the ones to come. She took many burdens upon herself while Edgar busiest himself in other matters. She cared for the children, saved money as best as she could and worked tirelessly as her husband's helper.

Rev. Seth R. Gordon D.D.

"My Christian wife helped me much as she was strong in the faith. No one aside from my dear wife knows the sacrifices we made to help on with the church," Edgar writes.

When it was finally time to lay some objects in the cornerstone for the new edifice, the whole Frost family participated in the ceremony. Thomas, 18 months old, put a Bible inside the box. Young James and Ella carried the box up to the church foundation, and Hannah placed it into the stone. Laura and Josephine had contributed a "paper" each, and one of the songbooks used in the opera house where the congregation met during the building's construction.

"This ending our work for a time," writes Edgar.

But he was not done. Already Edgar's darting glances and quick judgments were sowing new seeds that germinated even faster than the last, for now his heart knew how to grow them. Already he had chosen enemies in the new congregation. He seemed determined to mar their names along with Dr. Milholland's for all of history. Some of them were even of the same party that had met in his home to put the wheels in motion for the new church.

"P.S.," Edgar added to his personally written account of the history of Central Presbyterian. "In our church like all others some are Judas-like. Mrs. James Gray,

D. H. Thompson, his wife and daughter Mary Thompson and others turned back after they had put their hands to the plow. Others were afraid to come out and help because some of the rich demanded they remain aloof. Dr. Milholland, pastor of the First Church, acted in the most disgraceful manner even stooping to falsehood. This was a bitter fight but in all points I came out triumphant. Although many dead weights were hanging on me, but by the help of God I was able to conquer all of my enemies. Although it cost me nearly all my property and may take it all. Yet I firmly believe I am right and all will be well in the end. Many of my comforters were like Jobs'."

Although the foundation of a new church seems to have been built on bitter ground, Almighty God extended His hand to bring good from bad. The organization would go on the glory of Christ in spite of what certainly appears to be underlying distain for the wealthy, and also in spite of Edgar J. Frost.

Edgar's own story did not end there. He had set his face to the path of the bitter root, and it would catch up to him five years later.

2 | the story of the scandal

For some years, vague memories of the existence of an old "scandal" within the church history had been recalled. The nature of said scandal was never remembered. "But you can look in the old session minutes," had always been the answer.

Contained in the flaking, brown pages of the first record book of Second Presbyterian Church there exists one rather lengthy church trial, and it is the most scandalous affair of any following. It is remarkably larger even than the fornication and adultery cases just preceding it. Perhaps this just might be the event of distant recollection. Not surprisingly, it centers around Edgar J. Frost.

Since the founding of the Central Presbyterian Church, Edgar's snap judgments toward other leaders had chipped away the patience of his dear brothers and sisters. Nevertheless, they perhaps did their best to be kind to him. Even when Edgar began to show up to Sabbath services smelling of heavy alcohol and disrupting the reverence of the sacraments, they were willing to mind their own business. This was probably for the sake of poor Hannah Frost and the children. However, when Edgar began to lie in order to weasel his own way in matters, they were more than annoyed. When he started withholding his financial obligations to the church, they could no longer remain silent.

Edgar's manipulation had gone too far and had hurt too many. Besides, the church members perhaps knew where his money was really going. Edgar's sacrifices for the founding of the church had almost put him under financially, but now he was truly struggling under the weight of a much more severe power. If his alcoholism was not addressed, the Frost family and the church could be in real straits. It was their turn to let their festering bitterness erupt. It was their turn to make a drastic change whatever the cost. Whether or not they made the right choice, the reader can decide. For it does not appear to be a humble man they dared to challenge.

At a session meeting on April 7, 1898, the trustees finally accused Edgar Frost of "unchristian conduct." The church session resolved that his was a problem worthy of investigation, especially since the trustees had made efforts to confer with him already "to no avail."

In accordance with instruction left to the universal church by Saint Paul, Christians are expected to handle their affairs amongst one another rather than to take a brother to court. As was still common for congregations in those days, the Second Presbyterian Church would operate as its own court.

On April 14, 1898, in the case of the Presbyterian Church of America v. E. J. Frost, the defendant was charged with 1) hostility to the church and its officers, 2) untruthfulness, 3) alcoholism, 4) refusing to pay obligations due the church, and 5) insubordination. These charges and their specifications, complete with evidence and witnesses, were said to have been going on since the organization of the church.

When Edgar found out, the appalled defendant, who had fully developed the art of deceitfulness, determined to make the court proceedings as difficult for his accusers as possible. He immediately requested that 100 citations of the charges to be issued to him so that he could recruit and ready his own witnesses. It seemed he would be prepared to meet his foes with a vengeance.

On trial day, May 31, 1898, as soon as the meeting was called to order, Edgar objected to the presence of the session-appointed stenographer, Miss Lizzie Allen. He requested that instead, Miss Cara Wyatt serve in her place at his own expense. Miss Wyatt would furnish the session with copies of all of the evidence and proceedings as soon as the case was closed and it was convenient for her.

For the sake of moving forward, and continuing their custom of fairness to him, session approved Edgar's request. Little did they know, they had perhaps just stepped foot into the first trap of Edgar Frost's plan.

The charges were then read, and Edgar pleaded "not guilty" to each. After the testimonies of some of the witnesses, the proceedings had gone so late that the trial had to be stopped. It continued a few days later. This time, the meeting lasted from 9:00 in the morning until 5:30 in the evening. In the end, the defendant waived his right to make a plea.

The Christian court adjourned until the moderator could call the next meeting, which would be as soon as the stenographer provided the session with a copy of the proceedings and evidence. However, over a month later, Edgar Frost had failed to pay Miss Cara Wyatt for her services. Whether it was an act of defiance, the inability to pry his extra funds away from the bottle, or something else, the reader can only wonder. Alcohol addiction was not well-understood in those days, and the only real help available to sufferers who truly sought reprieve was the church. The anonymous, 12-step meetings for alcoholism, as they are known today, would not be created for another 40 years.

The session sent Edgar a notice that he was suspended from the observance of communion until the charges against him were disposed. Since he had taken it upon himself to not appear in church that week anyway, the notice was mailed to him.

Two months later, still no copies had arrived from Miss Wyatt. The lady informed Session that the copies had been ready to deliver for three months, but Edgar Frost had still refused to pay. To make matters worse, he had even endeavored to steal the copies from her so that the Session would be deprived their record of witness testimonies.

Another notice was immediately sent to Edgar asking him to comply with the terms of the agreement before September 30, or Session would proceed to judgment and Mr. Frost would incur additional charges against himself. This notice was personally served to him.

On October 1, 1898, Edgar still had not complied. Session decided to proceed to judgment. That day, they sustained every charge against him except Alcoholism, which was not fully dismissed, either. After all, such a thing is not always easy to prove. Edgar Frost was sentenced with "suspension from communion until he gave satisfactory evidence of true repentance" for his behavior. He was notified to appear before Session to receive the sentence, but that would be very unlike Edgar Frost, as we have seen. Instead, he "declined to come and suggested that the verdict and sentence be furnished him in writing."

Edgar soon appealed to the church session, but he had something else planned as well.

His letter of appeal was lengthy and very organized. It is not surprising that the very first reason he stated for appealing was for "irregularity in the proceedings." Of course, if Edgar had paid poor Miss Wyatt for her stenographer services that would have been avoided. The records are unclear as to whether the dear lady was ever paid at all.

Second, Edgar complained that he was not allowed to ask "pertinent questions," and that the moderator had told witnesses "not to answer" some of them that he did ask. Perhaps after an eight-hour day, people had been tired of listening to his drawn-out defense. This author in particular knows some folks who enjoy arguing. The reader probably does, too.

Edgar went on to accuse the moderator of being "unfair," of suggesting the answers to the witnesses, and of declining other important testimonies. He concluded that the moderator showed great prejudice. The moderator was none other than Dr. Gordon - the man Edgar had strived so hard to call to the church as their minister.

By now, the session apparently had grown so tired of Edgar Frost that a member of the judicatory even secretly expressed to the defendant a willingness to give him a letter of dismissal in good standing if he would just leave the church. Edgar J. Frost had no intentions of bowing out quietly.

Later that month, the Session finally learned of Edgar's next move. As it turned out, they had not been the only recipients of his grueling appeal. Redstone Presbytery informed the church officers by letter that Mr. Frost's case would be discussed at the next Presbytery meeting.

Struggling with the weight of the ongoing affair and now Presbytery's involvement, Dr. Gordon and the session met to pray and seek God's wisdom. After all, Presbytery had authority over their decisions. In the meantime, they also tried to visit with Edgar himself, if he would see them.

A verdict from the Presbytery came within days.

"The Presbytery reverses the action of the Session of said Central Church of Uniontown and restores Mr. Frost," they wrote, with the flippancy of older, wiser parents who were ending a meaningless argument between their children. Then to lightly slap the hand of the antagonist, they noted, "Yet the Presbytery hereby admonishes Mr. Frost to be more careful in the future so as to give no cause for offense."

Thus abruptly and completely ended the case of The Presbyterian Church USA v. Edgar J. Frost. No further misconduct by Edgar Frost, or anyone else, was ever recorded in the Central or Second Presbyterian Church minutes.

Poor Hannah Frost may have at times wished her husband had not made so many sacrifices to their beloved family. We could hardly blame her if she did. Perhaps she even harbored resentment in her own heart toward Edgar's neglect, alcohol dependency, or even his frustrating, brazen character. Not to mention what it must have been like to attend, or not to attend, Sabbath services during the months of his trial.

Perhaps Edgar's own wife was one of those comforters to which he had referred years earlier. In the book of Job, we read that the many trials the man sustained were, in the opinion of his friends and wife, a punishment for sin. Job adamantly declared he had no sin left in need of repentance for which ill fate should befall him.

Records show that Hannah Frost with her daughters and son James transferred their membership back to First Presbyterian Church in the winter of 1903, four years later. Thomas would have not been old enough yet to officially join the church.

The following year, on May 1, 1904, Mr. Edgar J. Frost also followed his family to First Church. His counterparts were probably all too happy to see him go. Perhaps it seemed to him that "gross immorality" being overlooked at First Church was not such a problem after all. Dr. Milholland was still the pastor there and would be for two more years. Dr. Gordon still led the flock at Central Presbyterian, which had now been reincorporated under the new name, The Second Presbyterian Church of Uniontown, Pennsylvania, as of September 20, 1903.

The Frost family did not remain in Uniontown for long afterward. Perhaps enough damage had been done, and they sought a fresh beginning. They eventually transferred to Doylestown Presbyterian Church in 1909, and from there most of the records drop off. Hannah died on July 5, 1934, and her son James was moved to the Inactive Roll at Doylestown two years later. He likely ceased attendance following his mother's death.

Thus, Edgar J. Frost disappears quietly from our history sources. Perhaps he springs back up elsewhere. Or maybe the events of his years in the two Presbyterian congregations finally tempered him. Through it all, he certainly left his mark on Uniontown.

epilogue | the reach of the bitter root

Long after the church split and the scandalous Frost trial, new generations grew up in Second Church and loved it. There were perhaps few memories of life at First Church or of the reason they had left, or even of the shocking case against a church founder - save for one notion.

One small thread of bitterness seemed to have survived, having woven its way through Second Church members. It was then passed on to their descendants. First Church, as is still the remembered consensus, was made up of only wealthy members of society, while Second Church was full of more "humble folk." This idea, whether true or false, would help to keep separate the congregations in mind and heart for the next several decades.

Some who remember when the churches reunited in the 1960s are still faithful members of Trinity Church today. Many say sincerely that all the animosity is finally gone. Others claim it still exists hidden away. There are still a few "First Church" and "Second Church" members left within Trinity, some say. Perhaps the old root really did defile many more than we could know, as the Good Book warns. But that is another tale.

Now if you, dear reader, recognize a bitter seed fighting to take root in your own life or in your own God-fearing fellowship, may you determine to stamp it out straight away.

Sources

Church Records:

Handwritten document by E.J. Frost (Fictitious Name)

Second Presbyterian Church Minutes & Register Book 1, April 1893-April 15, 1912, Pages 72-96 & 154

The Second Presbyterian Church Uniontown, Pennsylvania, Fiftieth Anniversary. Uniontown, 1943. Print. (Church Booklet)

the case of the tiffany windows

IT IS NOT UNCOMMON ON ANY GIVEN DAY FOR STAFF AT TRINITY CHURCH TO BE ASKED TO GIVE A TOUR. Cameras in hands, visitors will say, "We were passing through the area and saw your beautiful church. Can we see the sanctuary?

As the grand room opens before them, they marvel. Their first question is, "When was this church built?" It is almost inevitably followed by, "Are those Tiffany windows?"

"Yes," says the guide, be it the pastor or the church secretary or anyone else. "They were purchased at the World's Fair in Chicago in 1893."

This tradition about the history of the windows has been so longstanding that Trinity parishioners accept it as the truth, and they have good reason to believe it as such. They have the word of very reliable persons. Yet, like many Tiffany creations, the windows were never catalogued as being in the Tiffany exhibit at the Chicago World's Fair, and therefore, they cannot be verified. Without documentation or a signature, it cannot be proven that any of the windows are even Tiffany glass at all.

Let's see what you think.

The story goes that prominent church member Judge John K. Ewing was the most instrumental person involved in securing the cherished windows for the new edifice, which would be built in 1896. During the years leading up to the building, Judge Ewing busied himself scouting church architecture around the country and Europe to ensure the very best possible house for the congregation. He poured his own wealth into the project, and it has been said he is solely responsible for one third of the total cost accrued by the end.

On his quest for ideas, Judge Ewing, accompanied by the other members of the church building committee, traveled to the World's Fair in Chicago in 1893.

The Case of the Tiffany Windows

There, they visited the Tiffany Glass & Decorating Co. (Tiffany & Co.) of New York exhibit, which contained a mock chapel interior showcasing a massive stained-glass window display. The windows adorning the Trinity Church sanctuary today were purchased from the exhibit by Judge Ewing himself complete and intact.

If indeed a committee was sent from First Presbyterian Church to Chicago to attend the famed fair, there is no doubt this group of faithful were spellbound by what they found at the city on the shores of Lake Michigan.

The gates of the World's Columbian Exposition, known as the "Chicago World's Fair," opened on May 1, 1893. Over the course of six months, more than 26 million visitors thronged the 600 acres. The complex included over 200 buildings full of art, food, entertainment and new technological products. The fair commemorated the 400th anniversary of Christopher Columbus' first voyage to the New World.

Approaching the entrance, our determined group would have braved their way through the first exhibit - Buffalo Bill's Wild West extravaganza, a troupe of cantankerous cowboys and Native American performers who had set up directly outside the fairgrounds in rebellion to not being asked to come.

Once inside, their eyes likely would have been drawn high above the bustle of activity and buildings to the Ferris Wheel, the highlight of the fair and an engineering marvel. The 250-foot-high steel structure, invented by George W. Ferris, had 36 cars that carried 60 persons each. It cost 50 cents to ride, which was twice the price of a ticket to enter the fair.

Pressing inward, our Uniontown assembly would have passed countless pavilions representing nearly 50 foreign countries and 43 American states and territories. Exhibits included a full replica of George Washington's Mount Vernon estate, a century-old Californian palm tree, the Liberty Bell, a full-sized replica Viking ship from Norway, and a massive German artillery display that included weapons later to be used in World War I. Some of the products making their debut at the fair included Cream of Wheat, Juicy Fruit gum, Pabst Blue Ribbon beer, the dishwasher and fluorescent light bulbs.

In the center of the activity was a cluster of buildings with white stucco siding. The streets there were illuminated by electric lights. The area became known as the "White City," and it inspired municipal planners who were looking for ways to bring open spaces into cramped cities.

Only near the middle of the Manufacturers and Liberal Arts building would Judge Ewing and his fellow church members have found what they were looking for. Considered one of the grandest displays in the building, the Tiffany & Co. pavilion contained a chapel interior that demonstrated the firm's exceptional craftsmanship in producing ecclesiastical goods, including leaded-glass windows. It was reported that the chapel so moved visitors that men removed their hats upon seeing it. It had a rich, Byzantine-inspired look, full of arches and mosaic columns. Light filtered through the colored glass and reflected off of the mosaics. A 10-by-8-foot electrified chandelier, called an "electrolier," in the shape of a cross swept down from the center of the ceiling. A marble and white glass mosaic altar glittered at the front. The intimate space was even complete with a dome-shaped baptistery.

Louis Comfort Tiffany had begun designing windows specifically to meet the decorative need of American churches. Elaborate structures were being constructed not just in Uniontown but all across the nation. Tiffany hated plainly-etched church windows, and he had set out to create his own version of the brilliant medieval stained-glass of the gothic cathedrals he had visited in his early life studying abroad. He had also been influenced by the Byzantine mosaics and Moorish designs that he found everywhere in Europe. Now he was changing the history of glass forever.

The centuries-old windows of European cathedrals had been made of transparent "pot-metal" glass of pure color. The hand-blown glass with ever changing thicknesses became filled with air bubbles and other irregularities that caused the light to fracture and create a dazzling effect. Tiffany produced his windows with colored glass that was made in small batches and filled with bubbles and impurities. The production of his stained-glass masterpieces only increased with brilliance over time.

According to Trinity tradition, Judge Ewing and the building committee purchased the windows that adorn the current church sanctuary from the exhibit at the fair. This information is attributed to an architect by the name of T. Ray Fulton, a church member who remodeled the church's chancel area in 1950-51. It is documented that he told it to architect Don Heath, who added that around 1950, the windows were removed and shipped to the Tiffany factory in New York for repairs. The insurance for them at that time was $50,000. The original cost of the windows is unknown. What is known is that there is no complete published list of exposition windows available, and verification of Trinity's prized Tiffany windows is therefore impossible.

The Case of the Tiffany Windows

There is an incomplete catalog of the Tiffany exhibit which includes about 500 objects. However, it appears from a separate checklist that Tiffany had brought to the fair several hundred pieces of silver tableware, at least 500 pieces of other silver items, and 280 pieces of jewelry. Furthermore, Tiffany tableware with Columbian Exposition marks have been found that were not listed on any checklist at all. Therefore, Tiffany & Co. took more items to the exposition than they catalogued.

For this reason, it is still possible that the windows in question were in fact a part of the revered exhibit. However, an appendix of 1893 Tiffany products does list windows that appear in five Pittsburgh buildings. The windows at Trinity are not included.

Moreover, since Trinity's windows cannot be verified as Tiffany designs and are not signed, the mystery deepens. The "Christ Blessing the Children" window in Trinity's chapel contains a rose in the bottom left corner said to be a signature of Tiffany. But is that enough? Are the windows actually from Tiffany & Co.?

Only some of the firm's records documenting their works survive today. It is often difficult to identify undocumented Tiffany art with certainty because a lot of it was also not signed. However, as with most Tiffany works, it is easy to speculate. Even when there is no documented proof, Tiffany enthusiasts say his masterpieces need no identification. No one else could reproduce his style.

Trinity's windows have been accepted as Tiffany glass by art critics, including Tiffany stained glass expert Alastair Duncan. It has also been said that Charles Litt from the Tiffany firm oversaw the installation of the glass panels at the church from June 29-July 8, 1895.

Furthermore, it is mostly believed that Trinity Church windows are of the earlier Tiffany designs since they do not allow as much light through as his later windows. However, some of the remembered dimness of Trinity's stained-glass panels turned out to be a misrepresentation years ago. In addition to protective sheets of plastic that the congregation had placed over all windows causing a deep violet glow, the coal and coke era had also taken a major toll on the church building as a whole. The windows were covered with a thin film of soot. Over time, their dim appearance had become normal.

Even with the windows now cleaned and the plastic replaced with clear, bullet-proof glass, Trinity's windows are still not quite as well-realized as Tiffany creations in other buildings in Allegheny West. Therefore, they are still likely to be from the early Tiffany period.

In the 1880s, faced with increasing demand for windows, Tiffany had brought in additional designers to his firm, but he personally designed the early and exposition windows himself. Perhaps Trinity's famed windows may have even been personally designed by Tiffany himself. We may never know.

An 1898 history of the First Presbyterian Church says that Judge John K. Ewing's "contributions of money, time and thought to this building have been very large." It could be, as Trinity parishioners would agree, that this man gave the church one of its greatest gifts: the prized Tiffany windows brought from the Chicago World's Fair for which the church has been renowned for over a century.

Except, perhaps, for one window. The "Ascension" window above the balcony is the only window in the church with a memorial plaque. It reads:

> This window given in cherished memory of Eliza Carothers and Jasper Markle Thompson by their daughter Ruth Thompson Shepler." This window was said by J. G. Carroll long, long ago to have been "taken down and put back up three times before they felt satisfied with it.

It is unknown if Ruth Shepler, sister of J.V. Thompson, was on the special committee that traveled with Judge Ewing to Chicago. She was not on the building committee. How she came to dedicate this window to her parents is unknown.

Visitors will continue to come to Trinity Church and marvel at the awe-inspiring masterpieces set into the walls of the sanctuary, and they will still be told the story about the acclaimed Tiffany exhibit.

Most tales that have been passed by word of mouth throughout the generations always contain at least some germ of truth. At least we can be confident of that. The reader is invited to believe the enduring story of Trinity's famous windows as so many credible others did and do. The choice is yours.

The Case of the Tiffany Windows

Sources

Newspaper:

Miller, Donald. "Early Tiffany." *The Pittsburgh Post-Gazette* [Pittsburgh] 24 Dec. 1996: D1. Print.

Websites:

Maranzani, Barbara. "7 Things You May Not Know About The 1893 Chicago World's Fair." *History*. A & E Television Networks, LLC. 1 May 2013. Web. 31 May 2015. <http://www.history.com/news/7-things-you-may-not-know-about-the-1893-chicago-worlds-fair> "The 'Wild-Rose Vase,' 1893 Columbian World's fair Sterling Silver and Enamel Vase by Tiffany & Co., design attributed to John T. Curran, c. 1893." *Spencer Marks, Ltd*. Spencer Marks, Ltd., n.d. Web. 31 May 2015. <http://www.spencermarks.com/html/j66.html>

"Tiffany Chapel." *The Charles Hosmer Morse Museum of American Art*. The Charles Hosmer Morse Museum of American Art, n.d. Web. 31 May 2015. <http://www.morsemuseum.org/louis-comfort-tiffany/tiffany-chapel>

Church Records:

Copy of some pages of the "Official Guide to the World's Columbian Exposition in the city of Chicago, state of Illinois, May 1 to October 26, 1893 by authority of the United States of America" souvenir edition, compiled by John J. Flinn.

Letter from T. Ray Fulton to Mr. David Owsley, Curator of Decorative Arts Museum of Art, Carnegie Institute, Pittsburgh, dated 3 Nov. 1975

Information documented by church and community members in church archives concerning Tiffany windows

Brief History of the First Presbyterian Church Uniontown Pa. Uniontown, n.d. Print. (Notes left behind by the Rev. Dr. William Blake Hindman)

Trinity Church Tales to Remember

Dedicated May 8, 1896
Cost $150,000.00

the house of the promise children

THE SUN CREPT SLEEPILY OVER THE WHITE, WINTRY HORIZON ON SUNDAY, MARCH 8, 1896, but it must not have been difficult for members of the First Presbyterian Church of Uniontown to awaken. Although they looked out their windows to see a blanket of deep snow covering the ground and the temperature was below freezing, they dressed their best and started to Sabbath service early. Some arrived even a whole hour before it began.

It was a happy day; for it was the day they would dedicate their beautiful new meeting house to the service of the Lord. It was the day of the culmination of all their labors for the past several years. It was a day they would never forget.

People poured in the doors of the new First Church auditorium that could seat 600, according to the News Standard newspaper, although the architect had agreed upon a capacity for 700. It is difficult to tell which figure was more accurate.

Even with so many present, there was ample space compared to the Sabbath School room, called the "Chapel," which seated around 300 comfortably. The congregation had held their services there since January 27 of the year prior. Before that, they had been invited to joint services with the Methodist Episcopal Church, later to become Asbury United Methodist Church, since the fall of 1894. The generosity of the pastor and people of that fellowship would probably always warm their hearts to remember it. Now though, they were home.

It was not the first time they had seen the room. The decorating was completed a few days after Christmas, and the new organ had been dedicated on February 17 at an inaugural recital by Frederick Archer, the musical director at Carnegie Music Hall in Pittsburgh. Today was special though. It was truly the day when all would be completed.

Trinity Church Tales to Remember

The House of the Promise Children

Ushers showed the parishioners to their seats. The olive pew cushions yielded beneath them like silk satin clouds. Colorful sunbeams streamed through the Tiffany glass windows all around to reveal ornate details in every corner. Even the cherub faces embedded in the sculpted leaves at the base of the arches were said to be modeled after those at the foot of the Sistine Madonna by Raphael.

Gas and electric lighting further ensured that there were no spaces for shadows to hide. Among the relief work of the four arches were interwoven leaf-shaped bunches of incandescent lights, 144 total. Above the arches, a beautiful frieze was surmounted by a row of cherubim and 36 gas jets to light the whole interior of the tower.

In time, the congregation would decide that the arch lights too much resembled those of playhouses rather than a reverent church home, and they would cover the sockets with metallic, golden leaves. The tower gas jets high above would also cease to light. A story passed down by church members tells us that these were originally meant to be lit at night so that the lantern tower would be a spectacular beacon in the dark skies. However, they proved to be dangerous, or caused too much heat, or did not shine through the windows as expected. For one or more of these reasons, though we do not know which with certainty, the jets were said to have only been lit once and never again. However, on Dedication Day, supposedly all the original lighting of the auditorium blazed for a spellbinding effect.

That morning, there were few added decorations since they were not needed, but the chancel area was still adorned with lilies, begonias, ferns and roses. They added aroma and a wealth of additional color.

The whole place was magnificent. We can imagine that parishioners could not help staring at the finery before them, and above them, and about them.

If the sights were not enchanting enough, the enormity of the sound suddenly escaping the organ pipes was perhaps enough to send them into melodious bliss. The instrument had been manufactured by William Haskell & Company. It consisted of a pedal organ, a choir organ, a swell organ and a great organ. There were 2,138 pipes, and it probably felt as though each one was being used at once. These stood as stoic, metal soldiers fronting the tall alcove they guarded, their peaks of various lengths forming the shape of cresting ocean waves. They blew the Organ Voluntary like holy train whistles.

The piece had been a gift. Some perhaps knew, and some perhaps did not. The Honorable Nathaniel Ewing had proposed a new organ, and he himself had

Top: A. S. Milholland D.D.
Bottom: Rev. David Calhoun Marquis D.D. L.L. D.

purchased the grand instrument in all of its excellence of mechanisms. The qualities of tone and style had been carefully considered. Money from the sale of the previous organ could have been used for the new, but Judge Ewing had instead committed it right back into the church treasury. The new, glorious machine of music was presented as a free-will offering by the judge to the service of the Lord.

When the order of exercises commenced, Edward Campbell, the President of the Building Committee, delivered a brief speech. He then ceremoniously handed the keys of the church to the President of the Board of Trust and Deacons, W. H. Miller, who also gave a few words.

Dr. A. S. Milholland, the pastor, then made several announcements. He had hoped, he said, that the two surviving former pastors of the church could have been there, but neither Rev. Hamilton nor Dr. Gilson could attend. Dr. Ralston, another previous pastor, had just recently passed away.

"Death intervened and called the beloved brethren to the dedication of the house not made by hands, the home of God on high," Dr. Milholland said.

The rest of the service was full of more songs and anthems. Following a solo by Miss Sweeney, an unfamiliar man approached the pulpit. He had a thick brow, white hair and a long mustache that hid his mouth. His soft eyes crinkled at the corners as he looked out to meet hundreds of expectant gazes. He was the Rev. Dr. David Calhoun Marquis, a friend of the pastor, robed and ready to present the sermon.

He opened the Bible before him and read: "But the Jerusalem which is above is free, which is the mother of us all." (Galatians 4:26)

"Paul is here contrasting two covenants," he said. "One is the covenant with Abraham. The other is the covenant of Sinai. The first is of the nature of a promise. The second is of the nature of law."

Dr. Marquis reminded the congregation of the account of Hagar and her son Ishmael. Only Sarah's son Isaac was born free. He was the son of a promise. Both women had borne children to Abraham, but only Isaac had inherited the covenant with God. Likewise, children born slaves and children born free were both found in the Christian church, said Dr. Marquis.

"It manifests itself in every age and in every land," he said. "What Paul saw we too have seen and may see...the heirs of law commingled with the heirs of promise; the children of Hagar asserting a standing alongside of the children of Sarah; Ishmael claiming a part and portion in the inheritance of Isaac; the sons of the bondwoman mixed with the sons of the free."

According to Dr. Marquis, the first do only what is required of them, and no more. The later look for opportunities to express their devotion. Their motive is gratitude, and their purpose is to exalt and honor the name of the Lord their God. They do what they can and do it cheerfully.

But from where had they learned about Jesus in order to love Him the way they did? From the church, Dr. Marquis asserted. Saving knowledge of Christ - the knowledge which prompts such devotion – comes from the church. The church, then, like Sarah, he suggested, could be called the "Mother of us all." Not the building, but the assembly of saints.

"(The church) is the channel through which the life of God flows and touches nature's death and quickens it into newness of life. Why, my brother, had it not been for the visible organism established on earth, at one time in the form of a theocratic hierarchy, again in the form of a voluntary association of believers, but always in preparation for the coming Kingdom of God in the world, - had it not been for this, you and I would never have heard of the gospel of salvation. If we have indeed been born into the family of God, if we have been waked from the sleep of death and quickened with the breath of eternal life, if we have been redeemed from a covenant of death and made heirs of a covenant of promise and of hope, we owe it all to the instrumentality of that organic church where God's truth has dwelt from age to age and through which God's spirit operates in calling out and setting apart a people for himself."

We can imagine the crowd. Perhaps eyes glistened, breathing stilled to silent awe, and heartbeats drummed.

"We enjoy these privileges…" the minister said, "…and these hopes today because holy men of God have manifested their reverence for God's name and their love for his cause by striving for the maintenance of his church, by laboring for its enlargement, and by their gifts, their efforts and their prayers, transmitting it, the prolific mother of saints, from age to age."

As Dr. Marquis faced a people surrounded by the beautiful appointments that they had made possible, he might have waited, letting the silence reverberate. These were a people proved dutiful. These were truly children of the promise serving their Lord and King with joy and thanksgiving. Their building was striking evidence of that.

"This beautiful and costly edifice," he said, "reared and furnished to be the home of the church that is composed of the families who are banded together for God's worship and work under the name and title of The Presbyterian Church of Uniontown, is a fitting expression of the love you bear to that organization of believers which you are glad to own as the mother of loyal and grateful children."

It was true that their expectations had been more than realized and their prayers more than answered. Many were probably already reflecting on when it all started.

Now we will, too...

For some time, the congregation had considered whether or not to repair the third church edifice or to erect a more commodious house. Either way, they had to make a decision. There was feeble sentiment at best in favor of repairing, and a rather strong desire for a new building. However, no official action could take place until a congregational meeting had been called to consider the question.

When the people gathered on Saturday, July 5, 1890, Judge Nathaniel Ewing made the motion to construct a new church edifice. It was seconded by Judge Edward Campbell.

Captain W. A. McDowell asked what would be the character, style and probable cost of the building. Judge J. K. Ewing offered that he himself was in favor of a substantial stone building with all the modern improvements and appointments. All this met the approval of the congregation, and the resolution was unanimously adopted.

A building committee was appointed for the project which consisted of Judge Edward Campbell, Judge John K. Ewing, Captain W. A. McDowell, Dr. I. C. Hazlett and Mrs. M. H. Bowman. By Dedication Day, changes had occurred, and the names on the committee were then Edward Campbell, Judge John K. Ewing, Captain William L. Robinson, Morgan H. Bowman, John M. Core and the ladies Mrs. Rebecca Porter, Mrs. J. S. Schoonmaker, Mrs. A. D. Boyd, Mrs. J. A. Niccolls and Mrs. Samuel E. Ewing.

A soliciting committee was also appointed at the same time consisting of many of these persons again, along with other notables, such as William M. Thompson, the brother of J. V. Thompson.

Finally, a special committee that would travel with Judge John K. Ewing to the Chicago World's Fair in 1893 was made up of yet a different set of members.

However, no doubt many of the same names appeared in this group as well. Their task was to secure the best possible designs for the building, receive proposals and direct the general construction of the new church edifice.

Whether or not Judge John K. Ewing received recognition for his contributions to the edifice early on, he certainly received it in the souvenir booklet later printed by the church which contains the details of the erection of the new building. The unknown writer of the booklet claims that John K. Ewing "gave the matter all the attention, and was indeed most assiduous in his efforts to secure the most suitable plans, the most chaste and beautiful architecture, ornamentation, decoration, finish and furniture, the most substantial construction and with the most economical, considering the character of the house, the quality of the material, style and excellence of workmanship."

Although the church members had been excited for the endeavor, there was no particular rush in pushing forward. They took their time soliciting funds and receiving and carefully considering designs.

At last, on June 20, 1892, the plans submitted by Pittsburgh architect William Kauffman were adopted at a congregational meeting. Mr. Kauffman would have been given all the findings from Judge Ewing's special committee. In the end, the new building, according to Trinity Church members, was to be modeled after the Trinity Church in Boston – a structure that was consecrated in 1877 and considered by many to be the masterpiece of church architecture in America. The Boston church architect had been H. H. Richardson himself, and the building is a free rendering of the eleventh-century French Romanesque. The tower, its feature that most reminds us of Trinity Church in Uniontown, is an adaptation of one found on the Old Cathedral in Salamanca, Spain.

Now it was time to secure a builder. Sealed proposals were received, and the contract was awarded to the lowest bidder, Mr. H. L. Kreusler of Pittsburgh. He sublet the stone and brick work to Mr. Rees Lindsey & Co., also of Pittsburgh.

Meanwhile, the property of the third edifice was sold to Professor Griffith, but it soon passed into the hands of the Central Presbyterian Church. First Church continued to meet there until a lease expired, and then they were welcomed to join in worship with the Methodists.

Ground for the foundation of the new structure was first broken in the middle of the winter of 1894. It was January, but the excavations were started nonetheless. The earth was likely rigid beneath the workers feet. Some days they must have wondered, as we do during our Southwestern Pennsylvania winters, if they would ever be warm again.

This part of the project was extensive, especially on the south side, and at every location where there would be heavy piers to support the arches. Once, it became necessary to cut through a coal bed three feet in thickness, and this incurred additional expense. Finally, at nearly 20 feet below the surface, the first foundation stone was laid on April 22, 1894. The stones used were Peninsula blue sandstone that was quarried near Cleveland, Ohio.

A cornerstone ceremony was held two months later on June 16. After that, the work pushed steadily forward with no other mishaps or interruptions, except for a few days, and sometimes parts of days, of wet or inclement weather.

All total, the cost of building the new Presbyterian Church meeting house came to about $150,000.

When Mr. Kreusler's contact was finished, it had not included windows, decorations, seating, furnishing or a heating apparatus. These were provided in due time.

The stone carvings above the front entrance door were by Mr. Van Malderen of Pittsburgh, who also designed and put in place the stereo-relief work. The interior decorations were by the Bryant Brothers of Columbus, Ohio. The Spanish tile roof was by Scott & White of Pittsburgh. The mosaic floors were put in by Detrick & Merick of Pittsburgh. The woodwork was all by Titus Berger & Son of Pittsburgh. The heating and ventilating apparatus was by Peck, Williams & Co. of Cincinnati, Ohio. The electric and gas illumination was by J. F. Seaman of Uniontown with the electric wiring done by G. T. Evans & Co. of Pittsburgh. The plumbing was by Folsom Bros of Pittsburgh. The light fixtures were from Archer & Pencoast Co. of New York. The pews and pulpit furniture were made by George Faulkaher of Cleveland, Ohio. The silk satin pew cushions were made by Sperry & Beale in New York. Finally, the carpets were made by W. & J. Sloane of New York.

When it came to furnishings, the women of the church were more than willing and ready to make a most significant mark on the interior of the building. They began a Ladies Furnishing Society, which became a forerunner of the Women's Association. Mrs. A. S. Milholland was the first president, and the officers changed through the years.

Through sewing, cooking, holding a bazaar, and performing various entertainments including a mock trial, the society raised $3,076.82. Recollections passed down and then written and kept in the church history files tell us that "Mrs. Ewing and Mrs. Work stood at the stove," probably still in the third church building, and "fried oysters until their faces were burned turkeys." All food used had been donated, and the ladies charged 50 cents for a dinner. The Young Ladies Circle helped as well.

With this money, the ladies purchased a range for the kitchen, cooking utensils, tables, dining room tables, chairs, silver china, window blinds, infant chairs, the pulpit, pulpit furniture, and furniture for the pastor's study. In the end, they even had a small balance left over.

As the church members sat in the auditorium on the day of the building dedication, they probably enjoyed each moment. They would perhaps always recall with glad and grateful hearts the goodness and loving kindness of the Lord for crowning their efforts with so much success. Now as the message of Dr. Marquis ended, they were prepared more than ever to set apart the handsome building to the worship and service of Almighty God.

To this end, the minister led them. Dr. Marquis presented his conclusion with all the dignity it deserved.

He said, "Long may it (the building) abide as the cherished home of a peaceful, a busy and a happy household, a place where God's honor will continuously dwell, where God's word shall never be dishonored or diminished, where God's Spirit will perpetually manifest his comforting presence and his saving power. Long may it stand as the home where a nourishing mother shall dispense blessings, while she receives the loving service of her dutiful children.

"May the coming generations attest that you, whose beneficence bestows this royal gift today, have stood so true to the service whose claims you confess, so steadfast to the faith committed to you by a long line of faithful and godly ancestors, that your children's children down even to the consummation of the age shall be found walking by the same rule and minding the same things.

"Then, fathers, children and children's children shall alike receive the welcoming approval of their King when He comes to claim our common mother as his Bride, 'Well done! good and faithful servants, enter ye into the joy of your Lord!'"

It was time. The congregation read aloud the responsive words printed in their bulletins. Hundreds of voices recited together.

"This house which we have been permitted to build, through the gracious favor of divine Providence, we do now solemnly dedicate to the service and worship of Almighty God, the Father, the Son and the Holy Ghost."

Now the organ pipes pierced the air again, and the people sang with them the beloved hymn, "Holy, Holy, Holy, Lord God Almighty."

There would be additional services that afternoon and evening. Dr. Marquis would return to offer even more inspiration. Local ministers were also scheduled to come for other services through the week as well.

Later that year on June 28, 21 infants were baptized including three sets of twins. It seemed their parents had waited for the new church edifice to be complete before having them baptized. The meeting house of the First Presbyterian Church of Uniontown was durable, complete in its every appointment, comfortable, and spectacular in adornment. It would be the site of many memories - of weddings, concerts, fellowship and much more. Above all, as long as stood, it would be a testament of devotion to the Lord. Generations to follow would know that such an edifice could have only been built by true children of God who depended upon their Father's mighty strength and gracious blessing.

How about you? Is that what you see?

Sources

Newspaper:

"The Temple Dedicated/The Temple of Beauty." *The News Stan♦ar♦* [Uniontown] 9 Mar. 1896: 1. Print.

Church Records:

Trinity Church in the City of Boston. Boston, n.d. Print. (Church Pamphlet)
    A Brief History of the First Presbyterian Church of Uniontown, Pa.: As pertaining more especially to the Erection an♦ De♦ication of The Buil♦ing which was set apart to the service of Go♦ March 8, 1896. Uniontown; Genius of Liberty, n.d. Print. (Church Booklet) Documentation of Church Building from archives

*Note: In a *Brief History of the First Presbyterian Church Uniontown Pa*, three pages that seem to have been authored by the Rev. Dr. William Blake Hindman (Pastorate: 1928-1953), he indicates that the services at the Methodist Church were not joint, though other sources say otherwise. He writes that the Methodists "invited the Presbyterians to use their Lecture Room or Sunday School room until the new church would be ready."

Top: Josiah Van Kirk Thompson
Bottom: Jasper Markle Thompson

j. v. thompson and the theory of the myth

THE WRITER OF THE MARCH 9, 1896 LOCAL NEWS STANDARD STORY THAT COVERED THE GRAND OPENING OF THE NEW PRESBYTERIAN CHURCH BUILDING IN UNIONTOWN NOTED A VERY UNUSUAL FEATURE OF THE DEDICATION SERVICES. No statement was ever made about what the church had cost or if there was any deficit left. In fact, there were no known liens against the building, and the contractors and workers were all paid. It was commonly understood, the journalist went on to say, that whatever balance there may have been at the completion of the building was assumed by a few individual members.

It is no secret that Trinity Church was once home to more than one wealthy benefactor. The grandeur of the building can be attributed to the generosity of these affluent parishioners. However, only one name is ever remembered. That of the renowned J. V. Thompson.

Therefore, it is interesting that no known church documentation covering the building construction even so much as mentions him. Were his contributions anonymous? Or perhaps this "well-known fact" is one of the greatest myths of Trinity Church history.

"The Coal Baron" and banker Josiah Van Kirk Thompson had built a financial empire at the turn of the twentieth century through the buying and selling of coal lands.

Before his rise to the top, it was obvious that he had a promising future. First and foremost, his father, the Honorable Jasper Markle Thompson, was the president of the bank that J. V. might one day inherit. Not to mention, Judge Thompson's example in both business and faith paved the way for his aspiring sons.

To begin with, Jasper Thompson had a remarkable character. It is said that he often made it a point to talk about his Lord and Savior with anyone he met.

He was known for righting wrongs, comforting hurting souls, praying with and for the sick and dying, and pointing everyone toward Christ. He was respected, honored and loved, and when called upon to do so, he often preached in Presbyterian pulpits. Jasper's example of living demonstrated that a man could be both diligent in business and yet fervent in serving the Lord. This God-fearing father taught his children all that he knew of life and faith.

In addition to having his father's example, J. V. Thompson himself was a student of history. As such, he became prepared to face the future with fearless resolve. He graduated early at the age of 17 from the nearby Washington and Jefferson College determined to be successful.

Later, when J. V. began to build his fortune, everything he did was big – the biggest Uniontown had ever seen. For starters, one of the largest showcases of his wealth became the new, high-rise home for the First National Bank at its angled intersection site along the route of the National Road. Since the year 1828, the bank's previous buildings had curved around the corner of Main and Pittsburgh Streets. J. V. made sure that the massive, new structure was designed with the same round feature. He also claimed that his lucky number was 11. For this reason, the new First National Bank Building rose up that many stories high to be the most towering superstructure in Western Pennsylvania outside of Pittsburgh.

When it was completed, the first floor and basement of the building contained the banking rooms. The top four stories were reserved for apartments, and the others in between were planned for commercial space. The state of the art, $1.1 million tower had 750 rooms, marble halls and four elevators. It was designed in the Italian Renaissance Revival style of architecture, and it still stands today as an awe-inspiring monument to Uniontown's coal era.

The next grand representation of Thompson riches did not trail far behind. A few years later, J. V. determined that his lovely second wife, "Hunnie," also needed a new home. The three-story brick mansion that the millionaire erected for his sweetheart on the western edge of Uniontown was fortified with 18-inch thick steel and concrete walls. Inside, the rooms were filled with fine furniture, ornate fireplaces and silk wall coverings. The floor rugs were imported, and art from Egypt, Japan and other foreign lands decorated the space. There were 42 rooms total including a billiard room and a reception hall. The remainder of the 1,800-acre property contained a detached, glass-domed swimming pool, a carriage house, a racetrack, the servant's quarters, and more. It was called Oak Hill Estate.

J. V. Thompson and the Theory of the Myth

The opening of the estate in 1904 was considered the greatest of all social events of the time. That New Year's Eve, 250 guests dined and danced the night away at the lavish housewarming party.

Yet, the last chapters of the baron's story are a sharp contrast to the glory days of his financial empire. A divorce from Hunnie in 1913 cost J. V. a tremendous $1 million settlement. The once poor girl from Smithfield, originally known as Blanche Gardner-Hawes, left Uniontown far richer than J. V. would ever be again. Nevertheless, she did not have much time to enjoy her wealth. Church records indicate that Hunnie died of pneumonia six years later in New York. Other sources claim it was elephantiasis that took her life, a disease contracted from an insect while on her 15-month, 33-country honeymoon with J. V. The later claim was confirmed by recollections passed down from the late A. "Pat" Pallini, son of Pasquale and Angelica Pallini, J. V. Thompson's head butler and housekeeper.

Meanwhile, J. V. had already found himself on a downward spiral. He was experiencing a clash with other known money kings: Henry Clay Frick and Thomas Lynch of the steel corporations. He finally woke one day to a financial crash in 1915. J. V.'s primary depositors had begun withdrawing money from his bank at an alarming rate. They were frightened by a government banking report. This was followed by endless lawsuits that would plague J. V. until his death. He was forced to declare bankruptcy, and in turn he lost his business and home.

Fayette County sold Oak Hill Estate to the Piedmont Coal Company with the understanding that J. V. would be allowed to finish his days there. J. V. eventually married a third time to Rose Maloney in 1929 and died four years later on September 27 at the age of 79, seemingly penniless.

Through it all, the besieged tycoon was always very openminded with a sunny disposition. He was also noted for having a humane character. Perhaps it was his faith in the Almighty Sustainer that lifted his spirits through the dark trials of his life. After all, J. V. was a dedicated, church-going Presbyterian. The flock that claims him has always been Trinity Church. He had been a formal member of their congregation along with his family since he was 18 years old. Some Trinity members can even point to his former pew.

The sections of each pew in Trinity Church are numbered, as there was once assigned seating for the Sabbath services. It has been said that the pew assignments were a matter of wealth. The front pew sections were sold for larger sums of money than the ones farther back, and the very last pews were free of charge and reserved for the poor. Therefore, the wealthier parishioners always sat together and closest to the front.

J. V. Thompson is documented to having been assigned to pew number 13, next to his son Andrew and across the aisle from his brother William. Contrary to what one might expect, the pew is not in the front. It is not even close to the center of the sanctuary. It is located off to the side in the north transept of the church and about halfway back. Could this be evidence that the "selling of pews" actually did not occur? Or does it tell us something else? Maybe several other saints in the fellowship were just as wealthy. Or perhaps J. V. had secured his pew assignment prior to coming into his greatest fortune. If that is the case, it just might account for why he is not listed among the big contributors of the church building.

We may never know what J. V.'s pew location means. What we can surmise is that his financial empire did not begin to take off until following his father's death in 1889 - and what a sudden and shocking transition that was for him.

While away on a business trip, Judge Thompson had taken a severe cold that caused a violent attack of pneumonia. He could sense the sickness would end his life and rushed home to his family. He died within five hours of returning to their arms. J. V. would have known his father to have declared himself ready to depart if it was the Lord's will to call him away. During this grievous time, the presidency of the First National Bank passed to J. V.

Twelve years later, the first stone was laid for J. V.'s extravagant bank building. He was at the height of his power and fortune then. The Presbyterian Church edifice had been erected directly in between Jasper Thompson's passing and this momentous event.

Talk of building the elaborate Presbyterian Church home had started in 1893. The construction was completed by the winter of 1896, the same year J. V. mourned his first wife's fateful, early death. Mary Anderson had been 12 years his younger. Their two sons, Andrew and John, had been born not long after the marriage. The boys were teenagers when young Mary passed away.

Although J. V. was already investing in coal lands by that time and was said to have been the titan of the industry as of 1890, it is possible that his wealth had not skyrocketed enough yet to contribute heartily to the church building that so persistently bears his name. Or, perhaps he just had other interests at the time and left the erection of the edifice to others. This may be evidenced by the fact that J. V. was not a member of the Church Building Committee responsible for the plans for the new structure and carrying them out.

Actually, J. V. Thompson does not seem to have appeared on any church committees at all, ever. As it turns out, he may have also left the wellbeing of the First Presbyterian fellowship to others in addition to the building. When Mary was alive, she was known for being very involved in the church. Her husband, on the other hand, had been elected to serve as a Deacon in 1878 but declined. He never became a church officer of any kind.

In those days, a person was often ostracized if they did not attend church. Therefore, regular church attendance is not always an accurate indicator of the character of a person from yesterday's eras. Although J.V. was said to have required his bank employees to also regularly attend a local church, perhaps he simply felt moral behavior would likely result if they did.

Pat Pallini remembered J. V. as exceedingly generous, giving special attention to Uniontown Hospital, the Presbyterian church and even other churches in Uniontown. He also claimed that J. V. was a very dedicated church member. However, Pat was born in 1917, and he only personally knew J. V. in the twilight of the man's life.

The reader can perhaps wonder if the hardships of J. V.'s bankruptcy enabled him to depend more deeply upon the provision of his Lord and to more intimately know His love. After all, Christ did tell his disciples in His Word that it is easier for a camel to go through the eye of a needle than for a rich man to enter the Kingdom of God, probably due to the choking lure of his luxuries and wealth. On the other hand, J. V., in fact, was never known to have indulged in gambling, drinking or smoking, even in his younger years.

Either way, having J. V. Thompson as a tithing member of the prestigious First Church congregation was likely a great financial blessing to the church. Perhaps he was simply not a major contributor to the building itself. Maybe not even at all.

In the summer just before his death, J. V. Thompson's remarkable Oak Hill Estate was sold for $50,000 into the hands of a spiritually likeminded group. The Sisters of St. Basil the Great also allowed J. V. to stay in his home for the remainder of his life. They then repaired and preserved the mansion and used the grounds to promote their goal of spreading Christ's love. Many of the buildings on the grounds and the rooms in the mansion were converted into places of reverence, such as shrines and chapels. The mansion itself is called Mount Saint Macrina House of Prayer at the time of this writing.

Even if the prominent investor did not purposefully help to build a place of worship in Uniontown, a legacy of his has still been used far beyond his lifetime for the propagation of the Good News through mission and community outreach.

If J. V. Thompson did contribute to the church in the way that many Trinity members and community residents have claimed for generations, then historic church records and journalists alike have left that detail to our assumptions. Maybe only J. V.'s ledger books or personal journals could one day be scrutinized by a diligent researcher in order to find the truth once and for all.

But if it was not J. V. Thompson, then who are the unsung heroes primarily responsible for the illustrious Trinity Church structure? Perhaps the answer to this may be found in another recollection of this volume.

Sources

Newspapers:

"The Remarkable Career of J.V. Thompson of Uniontown." *The Allentown Democrat* 26 Jan. 1915: n.p. *newspapers.com*. Web. 24 Sept. 2015.

"Coal Baron J.V. Thompson Left His Imprint on District." *The Morning Herald - The Evening Standard* Bicentennial Edition 2 July 1976: 11D. *newspapers.com*. Web. 24 Sept. 2015.

"A Millionaires Honeymoon." *The Evening Standard* 6 July 1976: 39. *newspapers.com*. Web. 24 Sept. 2015.

Robins, Richard. "Old Coal Kings." *Pittsburgh Tribune Review* 2 Jan. 2005: n.p. *TribLive*. Web. 30 Oct. 2015.

Website:

Storey, Buzz. "The Historic Fayette Building." *Fayette Building*. Web. 5 July 2015. <www.fayettebuilding.com/The_Fayette_Building/About_Us.html>

Publication:

Oak Hill Past and Present. Uniontown; Laurel Highlands Senior High School Visual Communications Department, 1980. Print (James Kennedy, Instructor)

Church Records:

First Presbyterian Church Register Documentation of Church Building from archives

History of the Presbytery of Redstone. Washington: Observer Book and Job Print, 1889. (Pages 114-127, 222a-222b) *A Brief History of the First Presbyterian Church of Uniontown, Pa, as pertaining more especially to the erection and Dedication of the Building which was set apart to the service of God March 8, 1896.* Uniontown; Genius of Liberty, n.d. Print. (Church Booklet)

Personal Interview:

Kim Show, Secretary/Office Manager of Mt. St. Macrina House of Prayer

Oak Hill Estate at the time of J. V. Thompson

J. V. Thompson and the Theory of the Myth

Top: Main entrance reception hall of the mansion
Bottom: Hunnie Hawes on the patio of the mansion

the heirs of castle stirling

And whatsoever ye do, do it heartily, as to the Lord, and not unto men; Knowing that of the Lord ye shall receive the reward of the inheritance: for ye serve the Lord Christ.

Colossians 3:23-24 (KJV)

IN THE HEART OF HISTORIC SCOTLAND WITHIN THE VICINITY OF OLD LOCH LOMOND, there stands a protruding crag called Castle Hill. Sitting atop the ancient bluff is one of the largest and most renowned fortresses of the land. Castle Stirling is surrounded on three sides by dangerous cliffs. Ridges of heavy forest ripple across the encircling terrain. Since the fifteenth century, this stronghold has guarded the River Forth as a loyal sentinel. Many kings and queens of old were once crowned within the stone walls. It later served as an important military fortification when high royalty no longer graced the court room.

There is an old tale told which begins in the green knolls of the castle's vicinage. It is one of many stories centered on a robust Scottish clan that had long made their home along the River Forth. Their name was Ewing, and they could trace their lineage down to almost the time of Christ Himself. This particular recollection begins in the early seventeenth century and follows a small band of the clan right into Fayette County, Pennsylvania, where their legacy still continues to benefit Uniontown residents and Trinity Church members alike.

The story opens with one William Ewing. William was a clan member who had become the lofty Baron of the Castle Stirling. For all he had ever known, and for all his fathers before him had known, life would always carry on as usual for the Ewing family along the serene river below the castle walls. A hearty people made up the clan, and none who had ever stood against them had yet prevailed. Although William could probably see that the Protestant Reformation, which had been sweeping Europe for almost a century, had now trickled north and caused tremors of terror in parts of Scotland, he never imagined the worst for Clan Ewing. William died years before the evils of religious persecution did in fact overcome his beloved family, but the lives of his children were changed forever.

The reign of the Ewing clan in the region came to an abrupt and bloody end in 1685. It seemed that no Protestants in any European country would safely escape a brush with the brutal opposition to Church reform. John Knox had been largely responsible for influencing the Protestants in the Scottish dominion with a Calvinist, or Presbyterian, outlook. Members of Clan Ewing had received the Gospel of Jesus Christ and become Presbyterians. They declared themselves brothers and sisters of God's Most High Kingdom, and the Lord they served was Christ alone. They would live peaceably if they could, but if they had to defend their faith, they would take the sword. As it turned out, peace was not possible.

According to tradition, the clan was forced to rebel against their enemies. For the first time that they could remember, they were defeated. Their chieftain was captured and executed. The remaining families were instantly outlawed, and some were forced to forever vacate their long-held home on the River Forth.

From the sloping, Scottish dunes beneath Castle Stirling members of the Ewing clan escaped with their lives. They took whatever valuables they could in order to start a new life elsewhere. William's six sons were among those who fled. These stalwart brothers were later known in history sources as John of Carnshanagh, Robert, Findley, James of Inch Island, William and Alexander.

These Ewing brothers and other clan members first traveled to the Isle of Bute, and from there they went north to settle in County Londonderry of Ulster in Northern Ireland. There, the defenders of liberty felt compelled to take part in the Battle of the Boyne. The year was 1690. William Orange had opposed King James II on behalf of the Irish protestants. This battle marked the complete overthrow of James and established the rule of William and Mary. Three more Ewing men lost their lives for the cause of religious freedom in which they believed.

Alas, bitter persecution still reared its ugly head from time to time in Ireland. The next generation of the Ewing clan would determine to move on once more. Around 1725, the children of the six brave brothers of Baron William's stock put on their parents' bravery and faced unknown waters toward a new world. The trek across the Atlantic was a six-week trip on a vessel built to carry 140 passengers. Finally, the courageous immigrants entered the Chesapeake Bay. While sunlight shimmered on the blue water, they perhaps marveled at the lush green lands around them that were reminiscent, at least somewhat, of home.

These Ewings were financially able to purchase their transportation to cross the sea and, shortly thereafter, to buy their own lands in the new country. From Chesapeake, the siblings and cousins bid one another goodbye as they journeyed away to explore separate parts of this exciting land called America. Different threats awaited them now, but they were finally free to worship their God.

Nathaniel Ewing, a son of one of the six brothers, headed north. Thirteen years later, his son George was born. George grew up to wed a young woman named Mary Porter. When the couple had babes of their own, they called one wee lad "William Porter Ewing." The Ewing family often recycled names in a very precise manner. This William became the first Ewing to venture into Fayette County, Pennsylvania. Our epic tale follows his descendants, who would direct the course of the yet nonexistent Presbyterian Church of Uniontown for the next century.

Many English, Scottish and other Scots-Irish families were settling in Southwestern Pennsylvania at the time. William came to the county as a surveyor in 1790. He later constructed part of the National Road in Brownsville with the assistance of one of his sons. He and his wife Mary Conwell, called "Polly," had a total of 10 children. One of these became probably the most influential member of the Uniontown church of all time. Let's see if you agree.

The Ewing descendants were now mingled with Irish blood, and they possessed the fiery determination of Erin natives. They had always been a preserving people, and their ingenuity, wisdom, faith and compassion would be a continued testament to the character of their family for many generations to come. Their doctrine of choice was still Presbyterianism, and it is possible that William's family members were involved in founding the Presbyterian congregation in their new home.

The first time a Ewing name appears in the records of the Presbyterian Church of Uniontown is in 1799. After having gathered together for Sabbath services for some time but not yet organizing themselves as a church, a group of Uniontown pioneers sought to do so. On September 30, 1799, they met in the home of one David Ewing, who later became the new church's treasurer. It is surmised that David was a relation of William, even though his name does not appear in Ewing genealogical records of that time. However, "David" was a name that seems to have been floating around in the family by then, and it at least became used as a first name later. Perhaps this David had chosen to be called by his middle name.

At the time of the church founding in 1799, the man who would become renown in the Uniontown community and the Presbyterian congregation would have been 5 years old. We remember him as the first honorable Judge Nathaniel Ewing.

Top: Nathaniel Ewing (1794-1874)
Bottom: Hugh Campbell, M.D.

It is not known if Nathaniel grew up desiring a relationship with the Almighty Father into his young adulthood, but he is recorded as having been baptized into the Christian Kingdom, along with his toddler son, when he was 31 years old. It was the same year that he lost his first wife Jane. The couple had only been married for three short years, and now Nathaniel was left to raise their son alone. It is possible that this trauma spurred him on to seek true peace from the Great Comforter. He officially joined the church in October along with his lifelong friend, the medical doctor Hugh Campbell.

Nathaniel had graduated from Washington College with the highest honors of his class. He had been admitted to the Washington bar before he relocated to Uniontown. In 1830, he was remarried to Ann Lyon Denny, the daughter of a reverend who pastored a church in Chambersburg. By now, healing from his wounded past had come, and the intellectual was growing all the more sensitive and empathetic due to the transformative powers of his Redeemer. Nathaniel soon became an Elder in the church he loved and would serve as such for the rest of his life.

When he was in his forties, Nathaniel was appointed by the governor to fill a vacancy left by another judge. He served the constitutional term of 10 years with integrity and was said to have been the best Common Pleas Judge in the State.

Following the term, instead of returning to the bench, Nathaniel decided to use his lawyer skills to have influence in the Presbyterian General Assembly. More than once, he was sent as a Commissioner from the Presbytery of Redstone. At one of these important leadership gatherings, a difficult question arose before the Assembly. It became apparent that no one knew what to do. When Judge Ewing stood up, all eyes were on him. When he began to speak, the matter was resolved in minutes. With this and other acts of wisdom, Nathaniel was revered at the Assembly.

By now, the man who had come to the Lord's Table for the first time when he was an adult had become a pillar in the Presbyterian Church. He and his beloved friend Hugh had determined to follow Christ, and their leadership both in the church and without as Christian citizens shaped the community of Uniontown. The weekly prayer meeting of the church was largely credited to their help. It sometimes flourished and sometimes waned, yet the two spiritual guides maintained this most important practice. They were also both Sabbath School Superintendents at various intervals through the years.

During his lifetime, Nathaniel acquired great wealth. Although he always endeavored to give to the Lord without letting his right hand know what the left did, it was impossible to keep secret that he gave liberally, especially to the poor. When it came to matters of ministry and his own congregation, his love for Christ shone. Most notably, he helped lead the way for the construction of the second church structure for the congregation. The Judge's fine example in matters of life, faith and devotion to the Lord were watched and learned by his only son and his grandchildren. He began the legacy of Ewing contributions to the church which transformed and sustained Presbyterian history in the community. For the rest of his life after receiving Christ, Nathaniel had leaned on God for his strength. He finally died peacefully one quiet Sabbath morning without a single sign that his brilliant mind had ever diminished.

When he was alive, Nathaniel is said to have resided in a building across from the Uniontown courthouse. It was positioned on the corner of Main Street and the alley that runs from Main to South Street. The south side of the house was always well cultivated when he lived there, as the judge enjoyed gardening.

By the time of his death, Nathaniel's son John Kennedy had grown up, married a dear lady by the name of Ellen Willson, and had eight children of his own. In occupation and personal walk with the Lord, John followed in his father's footsteps.

John Kennedy Ewing (1823-1905)

Although he had lived a childhood life of ease with his father's wealth, John had still determined to work hard for himself. From the time he was young, he often read the law in Nathaniel's office, and he graduated from Washington and Jefferson College at only 18 years old. Within four years, he was admitted to the bar and later appointed to a vacancy on the bench of the 14th Judicial District. However, he only served for two years. He would have stayed longer had it not been discovered that impaired health was a growing concern. He consistently battled with medical issues. One problem in particular was his diminishing hearing, a possible hereditary trait.

While John was still practicing law, he was known as one of the greatest jurists. His fellow jurists often called him "Nestor," a Homeric hero, for being the oldest and wisest amongst them all.

Other feats of John's business life included his Presidency of the National Bank of Fayette County and his Directorship of the Southwest Railway Company. In these endeavors, he had foreseen the future of the coal and coke industries and had acted accordingly. His wisdom always benefited the whole of Uniontown.

When it came to his membership at the Presbyterian Church, John alone is credited with contributing an entire one third of the total cost to build the fourth Presbyterian Church building. He is also remembered as the person who purchased the Tiffany windows at the Chicago World's Fair. John had been a member of the Church Building Committee. He himself oversaw the selection of designs and supervised the whole building process. He did this after personally touring the country and Europe to evaluate other church structures.

A souvenir booklet of the church from the time period reads: "To his generous efforts, more than to any other is the congregation indebted for this most commodious and elegant edifice."

According to a tradition passed down, John felt that the original stone arches on the exterior of the church building looked plain, and he decided to have the lotus flower of the Nile design from the sanctuary carvings and pews repeated on the stone. Even the fruit of the flower can now be seen etched into the arches outside.

John lived a long life and enjoyed the love and respect of all those around him. Although a tragedy took his life in the end, it was to the comfort of his family that he departed the world whilst enjoying one of his favored pastimes.

The judge loved and appreciated nature. He often took leisurely strolls to soak in the fresh air and the beauty of God's world. These walks were done in his later years with the assistance of a cane.

On one particularly beautiful May morning in 1905, John was taking one such walk down Fayette Street. He had been checking on some work that he was having done on a lot he owned near the railroad. As he left the property and walked east on the north side of the street, he came to the edge of railroad tracks which crossed over the road. Just as he was about to make his way across, the shrill screech of an oncoming train pierced the air. Being hard of hearing, John had not noticed the train until that moment. Surprised, he tried to jump out of the way using his cane for support, but there was no time for escape. In an instant, he was struck by the cowcatcher.

Thus, the beloved Judge John K. Ewing was ripped from this world at the age of 82 by the screaming 10:02, B. & O. train.

The community and especially the Presbyterian congregation mourned John's sudden departure. Within his own family, he was said to have been "favored as few have ever been." He had trained his children carefully, and his sons went on to claim that it was his guiding hand that had directed them into their own life successes. John's portrait was hung in the Uniontown Courthouse along with those of his maternal grandfather, his father, two of his sons and his son-in-law, all former judges.

Moreover, two of John's sons are credited with the final large, known pieces of the Ewing legacy at Trinity Church.

First, Nathaniel, named for his grandfather, became a Judge of the 14th Judicial District. He became President Judge later. In 1906, Theodore Roosevelt appointed him to be a Judge of the United States Court for the Western District of Pennsylvania. During his lifetime, he was also at some point the chairman of the Pennsylvania Railroad Commission.

This Nathaniel is credited by First Presbyterian Church records for having purchased in its entirety the first pipe organ of the newly built fourth church edifice in 1896. He himself was on the committee that in 1890 had recommended the construction of the new church in the first place, along with his father. He was also on the soliciting committee to help raise funds for the building starting in 1893.

Nathaniel Ewing (1848-1914)

If that was not enough, he also donated a piece of property on Wilson Avenue for a satellite church that the Presbyterians opened as a mission for the Slavish community. The fellowship had been holding meetings in the Salvation Army hall under the charge of Rev. Frank Helmick. It was called St. Paul's Slavonic Mission. The new building was of Victorian Gothic style with light colored brick and had cost about $6,000. The structure still stands at the time of this writing, with the cornerstone dating to 1909.

Even after the mission was dissolved years later, the United Christian Temple congregation purchased the lot and began to hold services there in 1959.

The year Nathaniel died, the beautiful brick home where he lived on Morgantown Street came into the possession of the Saint Peter's Episcopal Church (now Saint Peter's Anglican Church) located next door. The congregation later transformed the home into their Parish House. It also still stands. Therefore, Christian ministry has continued to take place in Nathaniel's home long after his passing.

Samuel Evans Ewing (1852-1939)

Nathaniel's brother, Samuel Evans Ewing, also became a judge and served on the 14th Judicial District in 1899. Similar to their father, Samuel was forced to resign due to poor hearing. He also served the First Presbyterian Church in Uniontown like so many of his family members. The lot for the fourth building was purchased from him for a sum of $13,500.

All in all, the Ewing contributions are numerous and large, and these are only the ones for which we have record. It is difficult for this writer to imagine what the congregation would have been like without them. Would there have been a congregation? What would the beautiful church building that we admire so much have looked like? If Judge John K. Ewing really did purchase the Tiffany stained-glass window display at the World's Fair in 1893, the church building completed three years later would have had to be designed to accommodate the windows. "That is exactly how it happened," say Trinity historians.

We may never know how often the above credits were publicly stated. Trinity Church members now say, "There was once a judge who did this, or that... I can't remember his name..."

Perhaps the Ewings wished to remain in the background that they might fade into distant memory, as they have. It may be just as well that these men cease to be praised for their many, generous contributions to Trinity Church over three quarters of a century, for they would not have wanted accolades.

The truth is that these once rightful heirs of Castle Stirling in Scotland who shared their wealth of stately intellect and wisdom in Fayette County had become heirs of a far better kingdom. That inheritance was worth more to them than any worldly wealth. Their gifts for which we remember in gratitude were never meant for our admiration or enjoyment. They were given to the glory of Almighty God, their Sustainer and Friend - the One who had led their indomitable ancestors away from religious persecution so that they might worship Him freely. Which they did, for many generations to come.

We are also encouraged to speculate about other, more unknown contributors who have gone before us. Countless other families also fled their homes in the name of the Lord. Many braved the perils of a watery journey into a foreign world and, like the Ewings, ended up being influential in the Presbyterian Church in Uniontown, or other Uniontown churches. They trusted not in the promise of physical freedom, which is fleeting, but in the promise of the Holy One of God. He was their source of extraordinary strength in the most dangerous of times. Their obedience to Him interceded blessings for their descendants.

Generations of these courageous people have carried the Gospel message to all parts of this great nation. It is by the resolve of faithful men and women of God that America both exists and offers religious freedom to her countrymen. Through their bravery, many of us have come to know Christ for ourselves.

Monuments of the devotion of past saints mount up from the hearts of every city and community. Trinity Church is only one of these. Unlike the epic story of Clan Ewing of Scotland, many other such tales are long forgotten, but their legacies have lived on. Their lives, and ours, all have their place in the Great Story, which is written with perfect love by the Author of us all.

Sources

Websites:

"Ewing Origins." *Ewing Family History.* Marilyn Prince-Mitchell, n.d. Web. 1 June 2015. <http://www.sandcastles.net/ewing.htm>

"The Castle Story." *Castle Stirling.* Historic Environment Scotland – Scottish Charity No. SC045925, n.d. Web. 1 June 2015. <http://www.stirlingcastle.gov.uk/home/experience/story.htm>

Publication:

Riddle, William. "Part 4: Nathaniel Ewing." *Ewing Settlers of Southwestern Pennsylvania* Vol 14. No 2. (2008): Pages 1-7. Ewing Family Association. Web. 1 June 2015. (http://www.ewingfamilyassociation.org/swpa-articles)

Church Records:

History of the Presbytery of Redstone. Washington: Observer Book and Job Print, 1889. Print. (Pages 114-127, 222a-222b)

First Presbyterian Church Register

A Brief History of the First Presbyterian Church of Uniontown, Pa., as pertaining more especially to the Erection and Dedication of the building which was set apart to the service of God March 8, 1896. Uniontown; Genius of Liberty, n.d. Print. (Church Booklet)

Personal Interview:

J. David Ewing of Florida

the name in lights

A N OMEN IS SAID TO BE A SIGNIFICANT EVENT THAT FORETELLS THE FUTURE. Some are good, and some predict great calamity. Ancient civilizations felt omens were messages from their gods. Solar and lunar eclipses and the appearance of comets were among them. Still, humankind has probably always looked to the vast sky hoping celestial lanterns could predict what was to come.

Sometimes they do. For instance, Christians will always tell of the Magi from the East who recognized the birth of King Jesus with the appearance of the Star of Bethlehem.

Over a century ago, a special display of shining lights raised high like brazen stars also seemed to foretell the specific future of two prominent members of Uniontown society and the First Presbyterian Church. After all, the possible omen occurred at a quite notable wedding service. Since marriage is a sacred institution of God, the Lord has been known to show up in marvelous ways at ceremonies that honor and glorify Him. Yet whether or not something truly prophetic happened at the wedding in this story, the reader is welcome to determine.

If you stand alone in the chancel of Trinity Church sanctuary beneath the shine of fractured color from the lantern tower above, you can gaze down the aisle of crimson carpet and imagine the old pews filled to the brim. The place feels holy. It was meant for such a thing as a wedding.

Looking around, you can almost visualize the building's memories play one after the other like ghostly projections. The first is Mrs. Samuel Ewing painstakingly measuring the aisle before the pews were put in. She insisted it be wide enough for a wedding party to march down. Then comes hundreds of grooms standing face to face with their blushing brides. They smile. They move their lips in recitation of their vows. You wonder who they were and what became of them.

Trinity Church as a wedding venue has continued to be a favorite to present day. Engaged couples inquire about uniting in marriage in the hallowed space. In fact, most Trinity weddings today are for nonmembers from near or far who admire the grandeur of the building. The church staff works hard to make the day special for those who have chosen to marry within the consecrated walls.

The particular service that is the focus of this tale occurred on a Wednesday in 1905. It was the most magnificent wedding in decoration and finery ever before seen in Fayette County. The newspapers called it "unsurpassed," and 500 guests crowded into the sanctuary despite that it was the coldest night of the fall.

The first thing they would have seen upon entering the auditorium that evening was an impressive display of lights glowing brightly from the chancel. Raised high for all to see, bulbous electric globes were gathered together to form a rather large, perfect 'G.'

The electric light bulb had been invented 24 years earlier, but large-scale central generating stations had only been opened since 1896, the year the church was built. Electricity was still new. Families living in rural areas especially would still not have it in their homes until the 1930s. The front of the chancel being festooned with greenery interwoven with colored electric lights would have been breathtaking. The 'G,' signifying the bride's current last name - brilliant.

With the help of a Uniontown newspaper article that was saved, passed on many years later to a Trinity Church member, retyped and finally given to the church archives featuring the fantasy wedding in detail, this writer speculates that the memory of it may perhaps have been similar to this…

As the clock approached eight that evening, Miss Della Pearl Gibson straightened the skirts of her Duchesse white satin gown. Mercury had fallen below 30 outside, but she was not thinking of that. Her bridesmaids fussed over the final details of her appearance while she focused on breathing steadily, in and out. She could feel each rapid beat of her heart through the tight bodice of point lace over accordion pleated chiffon and pearl trimmings. The diamond brooch felt a little heavy, and her matching necklace sparkled against her chest.

Now the white tulle veil with orange blossoms was being placed over her head. Someone slipped her a small bouquet of white roses and lilies of the valley. She thought briefly of the large vase of American Beauty roses that had been sent to her the night before with best wishes for her future. The bouquet had been the centerpiece of her groom's stag party. Her heart fluttered thinking of Frank.

Looking up, she caught the gaze of Mary Newmyer, her Maid of Honor, who smiled and nodded. It was time.

Della followed the girls upstairs in a jittery, silent and formal procession. Mary and Mrs. Author Gregg Dillinger led the way with swishing white skirts. Maud Hogsett, Henrietta Robinson, Ada Reiner, Mary Ely, Ethel Crockett, and Josephine South lined up behind them like a row of red velvet angels fit for Christmas tree tops. Little Bess Arthur Dillinger stood by her mother with a small basket of Liberty roses clutched in her tiny hands. She would make the perfect flower girl. George Merts Jr., the page, also held his little silver tray just so.

Della glanced anxiously out the windows of the vestibule. All the guests had been seated. There was not a space to be seen. It felt as though all of Uniontown was present. It might as well have been.

Mr. Frank Eugene Merts was one of the best-known young men in town. He had already been in the mercantile business for several years as the most respectable head clerk for Maurice Lynch. They sold hats, shoes and clothing for men and boys. His parents, Mr. and Mrs. William Merts, were from Cleveland, Ohio.

Della herself was the only child of D. P. Gibson, one of the directors of the First National Bank and a leading business man of Uniontown. Aside from her social prominence, she was known for her beautiful qualities of both mind and heart. She had graduated from the Pennsylvania College at Pittsburgh and at the Seminary at Washington.

In essence, she and Frank were the perfect match, and everyone knew it.

The organist suddenly began to play the processional. One by one, Della's friends advanced down the aisle leaving her and her father standing in the vestibule alone. She curled her fingers around his waiting arm and felt a soft pat on her hand as she closed her eyes. She took one last deep breath. Then on cue, her father pulled her into a confident, graceful step over the threshold of the packed auditorium.

Everyone was standing now, and looking at her. She smiled slightly. Chin up and shoulders back, she made her way forward, clutching her father's arm. The warmth of the room felt nice. It was filled with so many of the best dressed people in Fayette County all baking under bright, red lights. The bulbs in the church had been covered with red shades to cast the place in a crimson hue keeping in harmony with her deep red color scheme. White chrysanthemums tied with red ribbons hung on the ends of each pew and nearly brushed her and her father as they walked.

Out of the corner of her eye, Della noticed some of the brides from that year whose weddings she herself had attended. They wore their own elaborate white wedding gowns again. Other handsome dresses and flashy attire flooded the pews. Gems and jewels, staring eyes and Cheshire grins became a whirlwind. Della blinked and focused straight ahead.

The front of the chancel was a bank of palms, ferns and southern smilax, into which were woven vari-colored electric lights. Behind the bridesmaids and groomsmen on either side were two immense vases of American Beauty roses. It all looked so rich and lovely that she smiled wide in spite of herself.

Then in the center of it all and above the heads of her dear bridal party, now in their positions, was the perfect surprise for her guests. Made of red electric lights, a large letter 'G' for Gibson stood atop the display. Della could hardly wait until the guests saw the clever trick planned for the lights.

A pair of bright eyes suddenly met hers. Frank was gazing at her with such love, and she did not remember him ever looking so handsome. She wanted to race to his side. Nevertheless, she took one careful step at a time until they finally stood just beneath the Reverend Dr. A. S. Milholland in his big robe. He waited solemnly for the congregation to sit and be still before instructing Della's father to release her to Frank.

The service felt faster than she thought it would. She paid careful attention to Dr. Milholland's instructions, to every word of her vows and how she stood. As someone acquainted with being in the public eye, she knew just how to carry herself. Meanwhile, she shared tender looks with Frank as they silently assured one another every step of their nuptials.

At last, the moment came that Della knew would be remembered well. When Dr. Milholland had completed the sentence, "I pronounce you man and wife," the big display of electric lights above them flashed from a 'G' to the letter 'M' for Merts. As expected, the transformation shocked and awed the crowd, and Della beamed with pleasure.

The red lights twinkled in Frank's eyes as he watched her only and never looked away. He stood solid and cool with broad shoulders and a strong jawline.

He had a fair complexion and light hair that was always parted on the left and kept neatly. The picture of a perfect businessman.

That was what he was. A family of two could live relatively well on 10 dollars a week, and that included rent and wages for one servant. Oh, but she would never need to scrimp and save. Whatever Frank would do in life, he would do it more than well.

Della thought of the immaculate Oak Hill mansion that had just been built by J. V. Thompson. The millionaire was somewhere in the crowd with their other wealthy acquaintances. Maybe she would not have a mansion built for her, but the opportunities were endless. Frank would capitalize on so many of them. He was the most brilliant man there ever was aside from her father. She was so proud of him.

Della's eyes fluttered closed as Frank leaned in to softly kiss her lips. It was over. Now they turned to face the guests. She was married. It was time to celebrate and begin their lives, and she could hardly wait. With the organ piping the jubilant recessional, Della marched back up the aisle, this time holding Frank's warm, strong arm.

When they exited the vestibule, the frigid night air rushed over her skin and filled her lungs with a refreshing chill. Frank quickly put his arm around her and flashed her that bashful grin she knew so well.

Her Frank. Her husband. What would their adventures be?

The reception followed at the Laurel Club rooms. The red décor with light shining from red bulbs cast the place in a festive and glamorous glow. Roses were everywhere and filled the air with a dazzling perfume. Della and Frank sat with their most intimate friends at the bride's table while the rest of the guests were served in the ballroom. The luncheon proved to be elegant with an extensive menu. Over 400 guests dined away to the music of Frank Rutter's orchestra in the background.

That night, the couple was showered with over 300 wedding gifts. These included a magnificent array of grandeur. To begin, Frank's present to Della was a brooch with seven diamonds. Never to be outdone by anyone, J. V. Thompson also gave her a necklace with 60 diamonds. Next, her father presented her with a valuable house and lot on West Main Street. And from Maurice Lynch, she and Frank received a beautiful chest filled with nearly five dozen pieces of silver. Though the two were already from a wealthy background, it was like a dream.

The Name in Lights

An early 1920s postcard showing the Lyric Theatre where the State Theatre would soon stand. The Penn Theatre can be seen down the street.

At the end of the evening, the couple was driven to Connellsville. They boarded a B. & O. train for the West. They would visit Frank's homeplace in Cleveland for a few days, and Della's father planned to join them there. He would go with them to Iowa, where he had some business interests. Mr. Gibson would no doubt mentor his son-in-law when it came to business affairs. When they returned to Uniontown, the Merts' would settle into their home with Della's father on the second floor of J. V. Thompson's skyscraper.

On the train, the evening's excitement buzzed in Della's mind and swelled her heart. Little did she know that the splendid wedding was only the beginning of the fabulous spotlight for the Merts couple. As they would soon discover, many more lights were on their way.

In 1910, Frank Merts retired from active business. But as he had worked diligently in the clothing store on the corner of Main and Broadway, later called Beeson, in the heart of the business district of the city, he probably took great notice of what was happening right next door. Ground had been broken for an imposing new structure. Frank and every other Uniontown citizen would have watched as a new, expensive picture palace was built right before their eyes.

On November 16, 1914, the Penn Theatre opened. Its design and architectural beauty had not been matched, according to the Uniontown newspapers. A single painting in the building had cost $2,500. The journalists boasted that sightseers would not have seen the entire city unless a visit was paid to the Penn for a motion picture. The opening show was "Cabiria," and crowds packed the 1000-seat house.

For a whole year, Frank watched the money rolling in by the thousands. He would have now understood the fortune to be had in the entertainment business, and he perhaps bided his time for an opportunity to join in.

That November, he seized his chance. Like a shooting star racing across the skies so fast you almost miss it, Frank suddenly became one of the four owners of the Penn Amusement company. It was composed of the Penn Theatre, the Penn Delicatessen and the Penn cigar store. He bought his share from Frank G. Monaghan, who was retiring to work in his cigar business, for a total of $65,000 - nearly half of which Frank paid in cash. The deal was the most important one in Uniontown during that year and involved a greater amount than any other real estate transaction in the city.

From that time on, Frank's name - as well as the other three owners, C. H. Gorley; O. M. Boughner; and J. R. G. Boughner - was surely up in lights. The Boughner's were also members of First Presbyterian Church with Frank.

By this time, Frank and Della had a 7-year-old daughter named Danna. History sources cannot agree whether her name had one 'n' or two, but she would grow up in the flashing lights of the theatre world.

At the beginning of the Roaring Twenties, the Penn Theatre and Amusement Company, as it was then called, decided to take on an even bigger, better project. The owners requested sealed proposals for the excavation of a new theatre building at the site of the Lyric Theatre and the Gorley building. This location was right down the block from the Penn. The company had commissioned Thomas W. Lamb to design the new picture palace. He was an architect known for fine acoustical planning for theatres of the day. The contract was awarded to the firm of the Bowman Brothers of McKeesport, and once the work for the new theatre began, it did not let up.

On October 30, 1922, the State Theatre opened its doors. The building had involved a cost in excess of $800,000, double that of the Penn. The State seated 2,000 and had a glittering canopy over the sidewalk outside to advertise its showings. Some chairs from the Lyric were used in the upper balcony of the new theatre.

From that time on, the entertainment company became so successful that in 1929, they completely renovated the Penn so that it even rivaled the State in its new appointments. By then, they were now called the Penn-State Amusement Company, and they also owned the Dixie Theatre and the recreation parlors of bowling, billiards and pool that were in both the State and Penn buildings and the Penn Delicatessen.

In this era, it seemed Uniontown had become more than "the cross roads of Fayette County," as it was called. To Frank Merts and the other residents, it was the crossroads of the industrial East. The opportunities were unlimited. Uniontown's future was assured with the spirit of the people and the businesses which made up the community. The theatres alone brought thousands of visitors each year to Uniontown from a radius of 100 miles or more. From silent movies to Vaudeville's finest acts of the B.F. Keith Circuit.

Keith Circuit, the Uniontown theatres always had the most modern advancements. The greatest names in Hollywood appeared on the screens. When sound and talking pictures were first produced, the State was the first again to install that system of entertainment in Fayette County. The audience likely gasped when Judy Garland as Dorothy Gale emerged from her black and white, tornado-riding farm house into the land of colorful Oz. They perhaps wept, awestruck, during "Gone with the Wind." The State also hosted the country's greatest musical attractions during the Big Band era.

It seemed that the name of Merts would go on shining forever. Frank Merts was an excellent manager for the amusement organization, and his skills and business sense had helped grow the company. Frank himself had also expanded his personal interests to be active in real estate and the coal industry.

However, all good things must come to an end.

One Friday night in the winter of 1938, Frank Merts was speaking with friends in the corridor of the Fayette Title & Trust Building, where he and Della had continued to live in an apartment for all of their married life. Danna still lived with them as well. Frank had just returned from a business trip in connection with his coal interest in Washington County.

All at once, the well-known entrepreneur was seized by a stroke. He instantly lapsed into unconsciousness. It was 8:30 p.m., and Frank was only 63 years old.

When he regained partial consciousness, his right side was totally paralyzed, and he was unable to speak. He improved slightly a few days later, but then rapidly weakened again.

At 9:55 on Wednesday morning, January 12, the end came. Della and Danna were both with him when death ensued. Perhaps Della watched the light leave his eyes as she remembered how a glint had always sparkled there from the time they stood together beneath the red glow of the electric light in its infancy only 33 years earlier.

The whole city mourned the death of Frank Merts. True to his Christian faith, he was a valued friend and associate of many. He had been modest, considerate and helpful to others whenever possible.

As O. M. Boughner had also passed away, ownership of the company was transferred to Charles H. Gorley and the estates of Mr. Boughner and of Frank.

The show went on, and the theatres continued to bring in good business, but the name of Merts was a little dimmer. Danna continued to live with her mother in the apartment until Della, too, and just as suddenly, was called to her heavenly home.

At 3:50 in the afternoon on Christmas Eve 1946, Della also passed away in the apartment. She had been in poor health, but her death came as shock to the town nonetheless. The Penn closed its doors that Friday, most likely so that friends and staff could attend her funeral services.

Eight years later, Danna moved from the Fayette National Bank Building, as it was then called, to 181 West Main Street, which is the location of Generations Restaurant at the time of this writing. This may have been the home that was given to Della by her father at her wedding. Danna remained there until she died at age 64 in Uniontown Hospital. Having been a teenager in the flashy twenties with all of the latest in entertainment at her disposal, and having survived the Great Depression likely quite comfortably, she had also been a First Church parishioner with her parents for her entire life.

Now the name of Merts in Uniontown went out.

Movie marquees were not given their name until the 1930s. Only in 1926 was the front door entrance of the circus big top called a "marquee." Yet the surrounding cache of yellow or white lightbulbs brightening the nights from the overhang of movie theatres eventually signified showtime, and then fame, glitz and glamor. They were eventually dubbed "electric tiaras."

Could it be that one of the first, primitive displays of these luminous orbs was used over 20 years earlier to foreshadow the future of the name Merts?

At the time of this writing, all original Uniontown theatres save for the State have now disappeared into to the past. Their lights have all gone out. Their buildings have been replaced or blended into the modern downtown façade, as it has been with the old, still-standing Penn.

The State has become the State Theatre Center for the Arts, and it still draws a crowd. The Greater Uniontown Heritage Consortium purchased it in 1988. On its stage, they present nationally touring professional productions. In memory of the bygone past, they also show classic movies. Prior to this, the theatre was used sporadically under the ownership of Clyde Tewell for presenting country and western music.

Uniontown may credit the existence of the State - a testament to a glorious time in its history - to the original owners of the picture palace. But Trinity Church members can especially point proudly to the faithfulness and fortitude of one of their very own – its General Manager, Mr. Frank E. Merts, whose name was first up in radiant lights inside their doors long before it shone in the glow of the playhouses.

Main Street around the late 1920s.

The Maurice Lynch clothing store and the Penn Theatre can be seen down the block from the State Theatre.

Sources

Websites:

"History of the State Theatre." *State Theatre Center for the Arts.* State Theatre, n.d. Web. 1 Oct. 2015. <http://www.statetheatre.info/history-of-the-state-theatre/>

"A Timeline of Home Electricity Use." *Energy Illuminated.* The Energy Consulting Group, LLC., n.d. Web. 1 Oct. 2015. <https://www.energyilluminated.com/timeline_of_home_electricity_use>

"Marquee (Sign)." *Wikipedia.* Wikimedia Foundation, n.d., Web. 1 Oct. 2015. <https://en.wikipedia.org/wiki/Marquee_(sign)>

Newspapers:

"Invitations are out for wedding of Miss Della Gibson and Frank E. Merts." *The Daily Courier* 12 Oct. 1905: n.p. *newspapers.com.* Web. 24 Sept. 2015.

"New theatre is Most Modern in This Territory." *The Morning Herald* 12 Nov. 1914: n.p. *newspapers.com.* Web. 24 Sept. 2015.

"Fourth Interest in Penn Theatre." *The Morning Herald* 16 Nov. 1915: 1,8. *newspapers.com.* Web. 24 Sept. 2015.

"Notice to Excavation Contractors" *Pittsburgh Post-Gazette* 7 June 1921: 7. *newspapers.com.* Web. 24 Sept. 2015.

"New Theatre to Start on Next Monday." *The Evening Standard* [Uniontown] 14 June 1921: 1. *newspapers.com.* Web. 24 Sept. 2015.

"Souvenir Edition Gala Opening: New Penn Theatre." *The Morning Herald* (Special Supplement Vol 23 #107) 11 May 1929: 21-28. *newspapers.com.* Web. 24 Sept. 2015.

"Wedding." *The Evening Standard* 31 Oct. 1930: 12. *newspapers.com.* Web. 24 Sept. 2015.

"Frank E. Merts." (Obituary) *The Daily Courier* 12 Jan. 1938: 6. *newspapers.com.* Web. 24 Sept. 2015.

the mystery of the silent tower

BELLS HAVE BEEN AN IMPORTANT PART OF LIFE IN MANY LANDS FOR HUNDREDS OF YEARS. They have long called mortals to awaken, to note the time, to pray, to celebrate, to take cover, and to take up arms. They have sounded freedom. They have sounded peace. Above all, they have gathered the saints together to worship Almighty God, Christ the Lord.

Bells have appeared all through time, but they began to take up permanent residence in Europe during the early Middle Ages. In those days, the clangor of cast metal had potential to strike deep fear. Men were not yet accustomed to their throaty tolls. It is even alleged that in the seventh century, the Bishop of Aurelia rang the town bells to warn the people of a coming attack, saving them not because of the warning, but because the approaching enemy fled in terror. The iron outcry was so foreign that the army wanted nothing to do with whatever formidable foe had made it.

Soon enough, bells were believed to have supernatural powers. In fact, when Thomas Becket was martyred in Canterbury Cathedral in 1170, it is said the bells in the tower above knelled by themselves.

By the 1700s, magical legends centered on the power of bells were plentiful. According to tradition, bells could heal, calm storms and drive away evil. As a precaution, they were rung at the time of one's death to keep the devil at bay while the soul departed. Condemned persons were even given this courtesy. On execution days, those sentenced to die were granted a ceremony, a small bouquet of flowers and a peal on the local bells.

In America, the established practice of a church bell came across the Atlantic with the colonists. A bell marked the beginning of Sabbath services in each community. Today, bell ringing is no longer the standard, but some churches still maintain the tradition.

The Mystery of the Silent Tower

For many years, a matter of much curiosity concerning bells at Trinity Church has existed. To begin the telling of this tale, let us cast our gaze skyward.

Rising 150 feet above busy Uniontown streets, the massive lantern tower of Trinity Church pierces our heavens. It mounts up to a pinnacle of the deep red, Spanish-glazed tile roof. The finial at the top is the *Fleur de Lis*, which means "lily flower" in the French language. It is found all through Louisiana and was used as a reminder of home for the French settlers of old.

The windows at the roof line of the tower allow light into the sanctuary, and at their tops, the floor of the belfry begins. It is enclosed on all sides by partially opened tiers of shutters. This massive space was created to easily house a large carillon - an instrument of at least 23 cup-shaped bells cast in bronze. The carillon player would be cloaked in mystery since no one, no matter how curious or how they strain their eyes, could peer into the belfry from the ground below. The only way to do so would be to climb up the broad, wooden ladder of the bell turret. The bell turret was also built to accommodate a church bell of great size.

But no one has ever heard the tolling of bells from Trinity tower. In fact, one of the greatest mysteries of Trinity Church is that the magnificent belfry and bell tower are, and for the most part always have been, completely silent.

In all of the full, known descriptions of the church building immediately after it was constructed, companies and individuals alike are given credit for their contributions to the church building, including the elaborate stonework right down to the dishes. One of these histories even includes the origins of carpets, the pulpit Bible, a clock, a sewing machine and a bookcase. Never, not even once, does the most comprehensive documentation mention a church bell or lack thereof.

The silence resonates into present times. When any Trinity Church member is asked if they know why there is not a bell in the tower, they always claim to have never heard anything about it. Except one.

"I recall hearing a story once," a thoughtful Trinity Church member once said. "But I don't remember it."

This man claimed that the late Judge Edward Dumbauld, long-time church member and master historian, once mentioned the mystery. If that was the case, the information seems to have departed this earth with His Honor.

The most logical suggestion that has been made is that the bell should have been placed as the tower was being constructed but the detail was overlooked.

Trying to rebuild the scaffolding afterward coupled with the substantial weight of a bell would make correcting the mistake nearly impossible. However, just one fleck of evidence may possibly contradict this idea.

Only one documented sentence concerning the bells of the tower has survived the passage of time. The unknown author was apparently writing a history of the church or maybe even a letter. With fair knowledge of the past, he or she mentions conversing with a "Mr. Carroll," identified in another source as Mr. J. G. Carroll, the treasurer for the Sunday School for 53 years, and a "Mrs. Clark," who both remembered events and notable people of the church history in the late 1800s. The writer also spent enough time within the church walls to "place new books" and welcome passersby who wished to see the inside.

The line, from the only surviving page of this old history boasting of the structure's grandeur, reads:

How many of you know that the tower is all rea♦y for a bell or carillon, an♦ ♦o you notice the gargoyles carve♦ high up on the tower in ol♦ worl♦ fashion.

The words can be dated to at least 1908, as the writer also mentions an event of that year. Perhaps we can conclude that at least 12 years after the erection of the church building, the writer still considered the bell tower "all ready" for bells. This seems to show no indication that a bell was not expected but rather that the proud congregation still anticipated its addition.

I will note that the tower did ring once. The sound began to be produced from the tall peaks in the spring of 1960 just in time for Easter. It ended during the Reverend Dr. John K. Sharp's pastorate (1981-2000). However, it was not the peal of beautiful bells showering down on the city below with the thunder and tinkling mist of a musical waterfall. It was the mechanical sound of electronic bells with speakers facing the streets. All that remains now is a faded plaque that reads:

Coronation Carillon
In Memory of George H. Bortz De♦icate♦ April 3, 1960

This was a Schulmerich Coronation Carillon automatic bell player that would have resembled a giant, old-school radio with knobs, switches and a clock face to set the timer. Electronic carillons were first manufactured in the late 1930s in Sellerville, Pennsylvania. They were invented by company founder George Schulmerich. Carillons of this kind could be played manually from the organ console inside the church, and they also came with pre-recorded hymns. The carillonic bells placed in Trinity's tower were given in memory of George Bortz through a bequest in his will.

However, by the time Dr. Sharp arrived at Trinity Church as pastor, the sound reverberating from the Carillonic Bells was not what one would expect or desire. The electronics were nowhere near the quality of digital carillons later created. When the inner workings began to fail, they could not be replaced.

This was the only time that the tower housed a form of bells. It was a brief stint, and it does not contribute to the long-lived mystery. Where is the bell?

Consequently, if not church bells, what does reside in the abstruse belfry so far removed from the world below and the changes of time?

Aside from a rare visit from an electrician, roofer or brave church member through the years, only the birds have frequented the tower tops. Pigeons once made their homes in the vast maze of rafters or down inside the smaller bell turret. Protective mesh has since kept them from roosting in these spots now, but evidence of their long reign remains. Residue of old droppings still splatter the walls and ladder rungs inside the turret all the way to the bottom.

The late Joe Simon, longtime church member, used to tell a story about an instance when one of these feathery critters died while inside the narrow tower. The bird fell all the way to the floor below, bumping and flipping an important and unknown switch along the way. This cut the main power for some of the sanctuary lighting. It took the congregation quite a while to figure out why the lights would not work and to realize the culprit.

Birds still frequent the tower for a rest, but they come and go as they please. There are more permanent residents that have lived on the rooftops since the time the church was built. Lining the hollow tower, Trinity's gargoyles are often left out of the church history literature as well.

Gargoyles were regularly posted at the tops of great cathedrals and other buildings as open-mouthed spouts to convey water away from the walls and prevent erosion of the mortar. The length of a gargoyle on a building determined how far water would be thrown from the sides. These protective spouts symbolized elongated fantastical animals as the result of an old French legend.

The lore of long ago asserts that Saint Romanus, the former chancellor of the Merovingian King Clotaire II, delivered the country around Rouen from a monster called "Gargouille." The creature had wings like a bat, a long neck and the ability to breathe fire. Two versions of the monster's demise exist. In the first account, Saint Romanus conquers his opponent with a crucifix. In the second, he is able to capture it with the help of a condemned man. In each version, the monster is taken back to Rouen and scorched to ashes. Having been a fire-breather, the head and neck of the beast do not burn. The people decide to mount the ugly remains on the walls of a newly built church in Rouen in order to frighten away evil spirits.

Thus, gargoyle works of masonry have been placed upon the tall towers of churches and other buildings ever since. Their job is to not only protect the structure from the effects of rainwater, but to protect the souls inside from spiritual evil without.

Trinity Church gargoyles protrude from lonely walls high above, but they do not include a water conveying function. Even though they have the signature wide mouths, they have never protected the building from physical deterioration. Perhaps as decoration alone these grotesques were placed high on the fortification exterior. Or perhaps the sentries of old were given another, more supernatural, duty.

Whatever their purpose, these stone monsters have watched the world change for many years from their lofty, silent posts above Uniontown. They will watch it still. Long ago, they even overheard the conversations of workers as they toiled away high above. They listened to the scratching sound as curious climbers through the generations have etched their names into the underbelly of the steeple to leave their mark on the magnificent edifice. Few others have seen the gargoyles up close. They stand as abiding guards flanking what was once to be the home of the grandest of bells.

Maybe they wonder, as we do, what ever happened to the bell? Or perhaps they alone remember the secret.

Sources

Newspaper:

"A Temple of Beauty." *The News Standard* [Uniontown] 9 Mar. 1896: 1. Print.

Websites:

"History of Bell Ringing." *Discover Bell Ringing.* n.d. Web. 1 July 2015. <http://www.belllringing.org/history/>

"Fleur de Lis History." French Quarter Market. *FrenchQuarterMarket.com*, n.d. Web. 10 Nov. 2015. <http://www.frenchquartermarket.com/history-fleur-de-lis.aspx>

"History: Birthplace of the Electronic Carillon." *Schulmerich.* Schulmerich Bells, LLC. Web. 1 July 2015. <http://schulmerichbells.com/about-us/history/>

Kurt. "Gargoyles" *Travel To Eat.* 5 July 2012. Web. 1 July 2015. <http://traveltoeat.com/gargoyles/>

Personal Interviews:

Gary Garletts, former Director of Music at Trinity United Presbyterian Church, Uniontown

Rev. Dr. John Sharp, Pastor Emeritus of Trinity United Presbyterian Church, Uniontown

a trinity house ghost story

IN THE LIGHT OF DAY, sun beams shoot through the stained-glass windows of Trinity Church like sprays of rainbow. Voices bubble up from the kitchen downstairs. The organ pipes eject their pious tunes as the player plunks the keys, and the pastor and secretary are at work in their offices. Even with the thick walls of the building, the noises of downtown Uniontown still penetrate the interior. The whole place is alive.

In the dark of night, everything changes. No matter how many bright bulbs burn, churches are still known for poor lighting, and Trinity is no exception. When the sun dips toward the horizon, shadows begin to fuse to the walls and saturate the corners of the rooms. Before long, blackness is trapped thick and deep by the deadened stone. The hollow-eyed cherub faces that peer from the walls of the sanctuary are eerily more noticeable. The daylight has gone, and another world has taken over.

Nighttime in any large, old building is a prime setting for a ghostly encounter. That is likewise the case when it comes to Trinity. Through the many years, there have been reports from individuals who were alone in the church at night but absolutely certain that someone, or something, was moving about in the building. Doors have been known to slam where no draft seems present, and soft footsteps have been heard fading in and out. Moreover, if there happens to be an unfortunate bat stuck inside, the nocturnal creature awakens to swoop and flutter aimlessly from the alcoves.

Often these unpleasant happenings are reported by organists who practice their music late into the sleep hours. For the most part, the creaks and groans of the great church are enough to frighten away even the most levelheaded parishioners. Rarely does anyone stay inside the building alone at night.

Yet for all of the mysterious occurrences at Trinity Church, only one specific ghost story has ever survived to be told. However, the spirit of this tale is said to haunt not the church itself but the manse next door, which was once its home.

A Trinity House Ghost Story

Rev. Dr. William Hamilton Spence

The four-story brick building still owned by the congregation was given the name "Trinity House" after the First and Second churches merged together in the 1960s. It was built from 1906 to 1908 with the specifications requested by the first pastor who would live there, the Rev. Dr. William Hamilton Spence. It is his ghost who is said to still reside in the place.

If you are curious, there is no need to wonder what Dr. Spence looked like in life. His large portrait still hangs in the hallway of the church leading to the pastor's study. There is nothing strikingly odd about the image when you first look at it, but it is actually one of the most disturbing adornments at Trinity today, now that those who placed it with love have all gone on to their reward.

The older gentleman is dressed in black garb typical of the formal attire he would have worn under his robe at the pulpit each Sabbath morning. He has fine, white hair combed to the side. Long wrinkles progress from the corners of his starless, deliberate eyes. The place between his black-hued eyebrows is slightly pinched, and the pallor of his skin is brought out by a hazy, darkish background. Although his thin, gray lips sit clasped and still, the trace of a tiny, uncomfortable smile may have eventually been on its way. It is when the observer begins to walk away that a peculiarity can be noticed.

This portrait is the same as Leonardo da Vinci's famous "Mona Lisa" in that the subject's eyes follow onlookers. No matter where one stands, or if they ascend or descend the adjacent stairways, they cannot escape the gaze of Dr. Spence. Although it is known that this illusion is created by light and shadow, the sizable, antiquated image of the minister with a penetrating stare can easily bring about shivers. That is why it might not surprise anyone that this same man is the subject of the only remembered ghost story of Trinity Church.

Let us start from the beginning.

Dr. Spence had lived an interesting life before making his way to Uniontown. He was born at Mossley, near London, Ontario on January 6, 1860. His forefather had lived in the Orkney Islands, and his own father was a Scott. His first pastorate was a small church at Kenora, Ontario. Toward the end of his time there, he married his wife Emma Oliver, whom he dearly loved.

A year later in 1886, Dr. Spence and Emma traveled to Kildonan, Manitoba, where he pastored the oldest Presbyterian Church in the town. It was a congregation composed entirely of Highland Scotsmen. By the time he and Emma came

Mrs. Milton Fischer (Cosette)

to First Presbyterian Church in Uniontown in August 1906, the couple brought with them two loyal, faithful and devoted daughters, Cosette and Helene.

In life, Dr. Spence enjoyed the outdoors and working with his hands. He often engaged others in intellectual conversation, and his love for Jesus Christ was evident. It was said that when he arrived in Uniontown, the First Church congregation was comprised of an elderly population. Dr. Spence worked meticulously to bring in younger families. When he retired in August 1923, the church had essentially become a congregation of young people.

It was also said that a large part of Dr. Spence's pastorate success had been due to the constant helpfulness of his beloved Emma. She departed this life very soon after his resignation from the church, and her passing mellowed and hallowed his remaining life.

Dr. Spence retired due to failing health, and he was named the Pastor Emeritus of the church in August 1923. He continued as such until his death on September 1, 1945.

For many years even into his retirement, the church's adult Sunday School class had flourished under his leadership. The group continued to study together even after their teacher's passing and still retained the name of the class as the "Dr. Spence Bible Class." It was they who requested permission from session to hang his portrait in the church. They were permitted to hang it wherever they wished. It has remained in its home on the wall outside of the pastor's study ever since.

There is also a plaque of honor which bears Dr. Spence's name on a front arch base in the sanctuary. It seems the congregation could not stop finding ways to honor this man whom they adored.

Three months after his passing, the session unanimously adopted a memorial to Dr. Spence which states, "He gave his life in faithful and fruitful ministry to us and for us, and we here record our love for him like to the love he gave us. We honor ourselves in saying we knew and appreciated him. The joy of his life will remain with us to bless us and to lead us."

The congregation anticipated that the memory of Dr. Spence would remain with them, but according to an enduring tale later told, more than his memory stayed behind.

The manse continued to be used after Dr. Spence's retirement. The last minister to the live in it with his family was the Rev. Dr. William R. Johnston, the fourth pastor to be called to the church after Dr. Spence. Dr. Johnston's pastorate ended in 1961. The church then used the house for various church classes and activities, and even the church office for a time. When the congregation became smaller and held most of their Sunday School classes and Bible studies in the actual church building, Trinity House was used for offices. Various agencies rented it through the years, including a counseling center. Due to later fire codes, the building's upper floors were eventually deemed unsafe. No new agencies were able to move in then.

It was during the period when the house was used for offices that a ghost story first emerged - at least to anyone's current knowledge. As people were on occasion staying in their offices into the late hours, it began to be reported by more than one person that they had heard and sometimes seen glimpses of someone walking through the house, back and forth, as though endlessly checking on all areas of the building after dark.

Had there ever been anyone who was so attentive to the buff brick home during their lifetime? The answer is thought to be *yes*. In fact, when the manse was being designed, Dr. Spence made sure that it was built with reinforced concrete. All materials were thicker than usual, even the plaster. This was so that the house would not burn, or would at least burn very slowly, if it happened to catch on fire. As it turned out, Dr. Spence was terrified of fire.

Perhaps he had a reason to be. There is evidence that fire seemed to mysteriously threaten him like a reoccurring nightmare. It was as though his greatest fear ever watched for an opportunity to harm him.

Just after the manse was finished in 1908, the foe of Dr. Spence seemed to mock his efforts to fire-proof the dwelling. On Tuesday night, April 28, a pile of rubbish waiting in front of the new house suddenly sparked to life. The pieces of wood shavings that were perhaps left over from the construction were piled up and ready to be hauled away. Instead, they caught fire by some mysterious means and burned quickly. The flames lit the streets for several blocks. It was almost midnight.

Fire Chief Wood told journalists that the fire would have caused considerable damage in just a few minutes if the department had not arrived when it did. Strangely, he also said that this was actually not the first time a fire threatened the property and also the church building. A similar fire had also sprung to life in the rear of the house some time earlier. To make matters even more peculiar, on their way to the second fire, the department's hose reel ran into a pole at the corner of Morgantown and Church streets, breaking the perch pole and front spring. Thankfully, no water was needed. Chemicals were used to extinguish the blaze.

These circumstances may have the reader wondering, as they do this writer, if perhaps something was not already plaguing the good minister before he even came to Uniontown with his deep-seeded fear of fire.

There are no other currently-remembered close calls for Dr. Spence, but that's not to say they did not exist. Perhaps there could have even been more mysterious fires from time to time that Dr. Spence was able to prevent or stop himself.

Therefore, it began to be said that the spirit often heard and sometimes sighted at Trinity House was Dr. Spence walking the halls ever vigilant for fires.

Not many people go into Trinity House today. Occasionally, a meeting is held on the main floor. It is often only the church sexton who ventures into the other areas of the old manse.

The title *Sexton* is an old name for an official of the church who is charged with caring for the edifice, ringing the bell and burying the dead. Since Trinity has neither bell nor graveyard, the sexton has only ever been hired to care for the church building's needs. The sexton is the janitor, maintenance man and the all-around handyman. He or she alone through the years has known the far reaches of the Trinity Church buildings, from the darkest corners of the basements to the roof tops.

When it comes to Trinity House, Christmas decorations and maintenance equipment are still kept in storage in the basement. The sexton ventures there often. The remainder of the house is seen more rarely, but there is not much else to see. The rooms are empty. Though when wandering through, it is interesting to imagine what life may have been like for ministers and their families residing there years ago.

A wide staircase winds along a front wall that is brilliantly lit in the day by a stained-glass window. The floors above are filled with many large rooms. At the end of the hall on the third floor is an area was once used as a grand study. It is encircled by wooden bookcases with glass doors. A door at the east side of the room leads to a porch overlooking Morgantown Street. The fourth floor is an attic with a trap door in the ceiling that opens to the flat roof above. Another, narrower staircase at the back of the house perhaps once used for domestic help connects the upper floors to a small, downstairs kitchen. Some items do remain in the few ornate, carpeted, and spacious first floor rooms. A beautiful fireplace with a mirror above the mantel, an empty china cupboard and elaborate woodwork attest to the original opulence.

At the time of this writing, the future of Trinity House appears bleak. Without the funds to maintain it, the beautiful structure may not survive to hold its place on Morgantown Street for many more years. Time will tell.

As part of his job, Trinity's sexton must occasionally scan the whole of Trinity House to ensure that it is still secure and no repairs are needed. Perhaps unbeknownst to each of the sextons since the 1960s they have always had supernatural help when it comes to protecting the old manse.

However, would fear of fire or love of the manse have truly kept the spirit of Dr. Spence from passing on? After all, the manse was not the house where he resided when he died. On the other hand, he did spend many of Emma's final years with her there.

What we do know is that while he was alive, Dr. Spence did reflect on death. Included in the memorial to him contained in the session minutes, some of his sermons and other writings were printed so that we might know the heart of this man who shepherded the congregation long ago. In particular, a preserved short story by Dr. Spence entitled *Our Easter Hope* is a tale of a chance encounter with the Spirit of Death. It was penned around Eastertime in 1923, the last Resurrection Sunday celebration that Emma would spend in this world. Whether or not Dr. Spence could sense her fate is unknown.

In the story, he describes a cold Easter morning in a lonely, snow-covered dell. The sun has not yet risen. When the narrator looks up, he is startled to notice Death passing by. Surprisingly, he is compelled to hail the dreadful spirit.

"Monster," he calls out, "of Thee no one speaks well. Thy tread, though soft and silent, makes firesides tremble, and in thy presence flowers die. No gleeful child is safe from thy all-withering touch; no parent dost thou spare; no lovers weaving life's threads of hope into fancy's colored dream; no Saint in humble prayer. Why not content thyself with beasts of prey? Why devastate our homes? Oh Death, I wish that thou wert dead!"

The being replies, hushed and haunted: "The flock must be gathered home; I am sent to bring the wandering to their fold; I give to weary feet the gift of rest."

"Why then," the troubled narrator objects, "is not a brighter messenger sent - an angel with music in his voice, laughter in his eyes?"

"This grimness thou alone dost see," says the spirit. "The living never see me as I am; only the dying see Death; what life is to the living, Death is to the dead. I am a mask."

As the sun begins to rise and silver gleams the snow, the dell is transformed, and the mask falls away.

The author concludes, "'Twas the Master's face I saw, bringing life and immortality to light."

Being a saint of God, it seems that Dr. Spence confidently believed that the Valley of the Shadow of Death for him led only to eternal life in the presence of his Lord, and of Emma. He left no suggestion of a return to this realm. Instead, he placed his hope in the One who defeated death for all time and who declared, "It is finished."

If Dr. Spence did remain behind after his death to keep vigilance at Trinity House, he neither planned nor expected to do so. As Job declares in the Holy Word of God, Chapter 7 of the book which tells his account: "As the cloud disappears and vanishes away, so he who goes down to the grave does not come up. He shall never return to his house, nor shall his place know him anymore."

But if it is not the spirit of a beloved minister who walks the empty chambers of Trinity House, who, or what, is it?

There is much speculation about the types of beings that exist in the spirit realm. I leave the reader to your own conclusions.

Sources

Newspaper:

"Small Fire Threatens Property." *The Morning Herald,* 28 April 1908: newspapers.com. Web. 6 Nov. 2015.

Church Records:

First Presbyterian Church Minute Books of 1923 and 1945.

Church documents preserved in history archives regarding Dr. Spence

Personal Interviews

that they all may be one

THE YEAR WAS 1961. Church membership in the United States was fast approaching 4 million. The country's new, exciting manned space program had started with Project Mercury three years earlier, and the Beatles were just beginning their musical careers. John F. Kennedy was the President.

In Uniontown, the First and Second Presbyterian Churches were cordial with one another, and many members of the two churches knew each other within the community. Their church buildings were mere blocks apart. They were "friends." After all, they were all Presbyterians and together under the jurisdiction and leadership of the Redstone Presbytery. Little did they know, their friendship was about to be put to the test.

This is a tale of a tumultuous era in Trinity Church history that is still remembered by some at the time of this writing. It is the story of how the Trinity United Presbyterian Church came into being.

1 | the story of the divided vote

It was a spring day when the members of each congregation received the notice.

"That They All May Be One" was the bold title across the top. It was addressed to the Communicant Members of the First and Second Presbyterian Churches of Uniontown, Pennsylvania, and surely to the shock of most, it posed the question, "Shall we unite to form a new congregation, with the understanding that letters of dismissal to other churches will be granted to any who request it?"

The document informed the startled church members that the PC(USA) was suggesting churches should be united when possible in over-churched communities, and Uniontown, having a total of 14 major white Protestant churches and a number of smaller churches within the city limits, was identified as such a community. It was believed by the two sessions, according to the letter, that the union would save money and that ample pastoral care and leadership would still be available to all. The first vote to determine if a merger of First and Second Churches should happen was to take place in both places of worship on May 21.

Dare this writer suggest that a personal attack, or perhaps even an attack to one's family or friends, sometimes does not cut as deeply as a threat to one's faith. Or even worse, to the home in which it has been nourished - that place of deepest, purest comfort, and the seeming holiest space a life will ever know in this realm. So very precious can a religious building sometimes become to human hearts that it is even on occasion dangerous to the life of a church. Everything from the Sunday school rooms, to the basement kitchens, to the smell of the old hymn books can ignite memories that feel stitched with supernatural thread to the very souls of those who lived them. To change or take away the sacred places would be to rip out the thread and leave a raw, open wound.

At least, that is the feeling as I can best understand it. That is why, dear reader, some folks might behave a little out of character when a suggestion is made for even a very minor alteration at "their church."

Perhaps the not-so-welcome letters that day years ago were thrown down on desks, passed around to wide-eyed family members, or even dribbled upon with a tear or two. Either way, their contents would have been the topic of much discussion around dinner tables, and everywhere else.

A Morning Herald newspaper story that year reported that the membership of First Church was 750, and Second Church was 832. However, there is much indication that far less than half of these numbers attended services regularly. For instance, according to the same article, 321 members appearing in Second Church at one time was considered "far above the average attendance." In addition, one current Trinity Church member who was present in those days had believed it was for lack of membership that the merger was proposed.

Be that as it may, the two church sanctuaries are remembered to have been very full on Sunday mornings, especially on Easter and around Christmas. For those holidays, extra chairs had to be placed in the sanctuaries.

Therefore, it is probably safe for us to surmise that the recommended merger was not on account of dwindling attendance, though it was likely a factor. What were the other reasons? No one remembers entirely.

Many Trinity members who were either members at the time or had arrived during the years soon afterward have indicated that it was not the desire of either church to unite, especially Second Church. Rather, it was a decision encouraged, very firmly, by their superiors. Each session worked to persuade their respective church, and it is believed that the Presbytery worked to persuade them.

"There was a feeling that the hierarchy of the church had really moved mountains to get these two churches to merge," said the Rev. Dr. John Sharp. Dr. Sharp was not the minister at the time of the merger, but he came next in 1981.

Whether or not there were hierarchical reasons for the impending merger that will forever remain a mystery, the factor most often mentioned in Trinity Church records is the economy. Both congregations had a massive, aging structure to maintain. Their numbers were beginning to decrease, and the glory days of Uniontown were far behind them. The people of both churches understood. However, it did not mean they were ready to join together.

Both congregations were not without clear foresight. They knew that many uncomfortable changes would need to be made in order to merge. One of the most important of these for the Second Church members was the matter of the buildings. When choosing what structure the newly formed church would use for worship, it would most undoubtedly not be theirs, which had less seating, was not as grand, and it would soon need repair work of its own.

The next question was: which of the two ministers would be the pastor of this new church?

There was not much time to contemplate though. The decision was fast approaching, and the likelihood the brethren submitting to the advice of their spiritual authorities was great. Still, the outcome remained entirely unpredictable.

When decision day arrived, parishioners packed their church houses and cast their ballots. The results were carefully tallied to reveal that First Church had voted yes, 223 to 42; and Second Church also voted yes, but with a significantly smaller margin of 187 to 180. Although the vote at Second Church was close, their session still persistently said they felt it was God's will and pushed ahead, recommending to Presbytery that a Plan of Union be prepared.

Actions to prepare the plan began at once, but it was a lengthy process. Each church had several active groups, such as ladies' associations, choirs, Bible studies and youth groups. These all had their own way of doing things, and agreements would need to be made in advance. In the meantime, to warm both congregations to one another and to the idea, joint worship services were held during the summer.

On September 19, 1961, C. Greer Bailey, Stated Clerk for the Redstone Presbytery wrote to Mr. Hansel, Clerk of Session for Second Church, and to Mr. G. R. Hunley, Clerk of Session for First Church, reminding them that a vote to unite the two congregations had been taken, but now it was time to vote to adopt the completed Plan of Union. It had been meticulously created with the input of eight members from each congregation.

That same day, a letter was sent from both clerks to the First and Second Church members with an enclosed copy of the proposed plan.

October 8 was designated as the next big voting day. When that morning arrived, the events happened quite differently than expected. At First Church, the people seemed to be even more comfortable with the idea of the merger than before. But another very large crowd had gathered in the sanctuary of Second Church. Members who had not been to services in some time had come just to cast their ballots. It was now or never to have their voices heard.

When the voting results were announced, the community was shocked to learn that Second Church had voted no, 133 to 188. "Merger Vote By Churches Is 'Divided'" read the headlines of the October 9, 1961 Morning Herald. First Church had again voted with a very large majority, 188 to 16, yes.

It was clear to all by this that Second Church did not necessarily oppose the details of how the union ought to happen. Rather, over half of their number opposed the merger altogether.

Not knowing what else to do, Second Church minister Wilbur F. Christy with the Clerk of Session composed a letter to the clerk of First Church two days later:

Dear Mr. Hunley:

The Session of the Secon♦ Presbyterian Church wishes to express to the Session an♦ Congregation of the First Presbyterian Church its ♦eep feeling of regret at the vote of the congregation of our church on this past Sun♦ay...We regret that the vote

> *of the recent Congregational Meeting of October 8 was not one of good faith. The vote was to be taken on the Plan of Union, but we can only interpret the vote as one of whether we should unite or not. Our Session is waiting for guidance from Presbytery regarding further action.*

As it turned out, although the Plan of Union was not approved, the first vote had already set the merger into motion, whether everyone liked it or not. The church officers would have to do their best to convince all of their members that the decision had been the right one. Both church congregations were at some point given a five-page memo seemingly from their church officers with detailed explanations for why a merger would help to preserve the church as a whole in the future.

"The day of fortunes in Uniontown has come and gone," it read. "Our community is fighting just to keep even, just to maintain a decent level of living. The dollar is harder to come by, and harder to keep."

With the economy sinking, could either church expect to grow? The document challenged readers to ask the youth of their congregation where they expected to live when they graduated from high school or college. Very few planned to stay in Uniontown. The grown children of most church members had already left the community.

"If the strength of our two congregations were united," it went on to say, "the resulting service to God in witness and nurture would be stronger than either of the two churches alone could ever hope to attain."

With some persuading, or perhaps second thoughts or changes of heart, Second Church apparently did agree upon a plan of union during the winter in 1962. However, several of their members asked to be dismissed to other congregations.

At last, the Consummation Service was scheduled for Sunday, February 4 that year. Not surprisingly, it was held in the First Church building. Rev. Carl Fisher, minister of the First Presbyterian Church of Johnstown, and moderator of the Synod of Pennsylvania, gave the sermon that day, which was entitled, "I Will Build My Church." Rev. Roy Brice, chairman of the Ministerial Relations Committee of the Redstone Presbytery, delivered the Declaration of Consummation, and history was made.

Thus, the Trinity United Presbyterian Church of Uniontown was born.

2 | the story of the divided house

The consummation of the First and Second Churches had taken mere moments. The literal merging of the two congregations would take many long years.

"It was probably a generation before it was accepted more," said one former First Church member.

Indeed, the effects of the union were even showing themselves as late as 20 years after the fact.

"It was a big deal. I'm glad I didn't live through it. Although, I lived with it," said Dr. Sharp. Even in the 1980s, he could still surmise that the two congregations had not particularly wanted to unite.

Directly following the consummation service, the new Trinity Church members started to experience drastic changes. Right away, it had been decided that retaining either minister from the two former churches would not be favorable, and the people had to say their goodbyes to both beloved friends. Rev. Wilbur Christy had only been with Second Church for three years. He was a young man and very active with the youth. Likewise, Rev. Bill Johnston was said to be a fun-loving man but with a serious side, and he always knew everyone's name and inquired about them.

The man whose job it would be to unite the congregations spiritually was the newly called minister, the Rev. Dr. Vincent T. Ross. Fortunately, he also became well-liked by many Trinity Church members. Dr. Ross was small in stature. He was said to be not more than 5-foot-8, and he was known for speaking to everyone when walking down the street. However, when he entered a room, he was also said to take over. According to the church secretary at the time, he preferred to be the leader of any endeavor. Perhaps this kind of commanding leadership was exactly what the divided church needed. Let's see what you think.

For although they were in the same auditorium and worshipping together, the two former congregations were still entirely separated in both mind and heart. They identified each other as, "She's a First Church," and "He's a Second."

First Church, in a sense, had been favorable enough toward the merger that there is hardly any evidence left of their negativity. A former First Church member has said, "Well, it was traumatic for both sides, of course. I don't really know much about it."

Whether or not First Church people were as upset about the merger, Second Church folks proved to be much more outspoken about their feelings against it.

"First Pres decided they wanted to merge," – is the remembrance of Mary Martha Lorenzo, former Second Church secretary and member. Mary Martha remained the secretary at Trinity Church after the union. She is still a member of Trinity at the time of this writing.

"Second Pres needed the money," she said. "They didn't have any money, so they merged. It wasn't a happy situation."

According to her, many of the Second Church members who chose to withdraw their membership transferred to the Third Presbyterian Church of Uniontown.

"First Pres was known as a money church. They wanted to stick by that. Second Pres was known as the religious church. They stuck more to religion than money matters," Mary Martha said.

First Church had been home to many lawyers, doctors and banking personnel. In contrast, Second Church had long been made up of retailers, and those who worked under First Church members. The friction was perhaps inevitable.

Mary Martha's counterpart, the secretary who had worked for First Church, had also remained employed by Trinity Church for a little while.

"She was strictly First Pres, and she kept it that way," said Mary Martha.

According to Mary Martha, the "First Church" secretary would not let her "Second Church" co-worker even look at the First Church registries and session minute books.

"She wouldn't let me have anything to do with them. She never let me forget that I was not First Pres," she said.

She also said that the woman would sometimes keep important church office information from Mary Martha as well.

Mary Martha said that First Church people often tended to stick to themselves. That was how they did their part in keeping the division strong.

Second Church, on the other hand, did it with their sheer numbers. There were more of them. In this way, they were able to direct the actions of the new Trinity Church – and they did.

Pauline "Robin" Semans said that First Church had often held bazaars and sales to raise money through the years. Robin is a former First Church member and is still a member of Trinity at the time of this writing.

"The Women's Association had special dishcloths and sold them," she said. "That was a project. They might have sold pecans at Christmas time. They had little charity bazaars where they had food and some clothing."

When Second Church people arrived, they held different views about those types of events. At least at that time, the church stopped holding the events.

Not long after the merger, Trinity Church sold the Church Street property. It was no doubt a sad season for former Second Church members. Their precious building passed into the hands of the Uniontown Parking Authority in July 1962. The conditions were that the organ, organ chimes and stained-glass be excluded from the sale.

When the structure was torn down shortly after, the cornerstone was returned to Trinity Church. It was opened during a special meeting of curious congregation members on February 27, 1963. The contents inside included photographs of the first minister of Central Presbyterian and his wife, copies of newspapers from 1895, copies of other publications, a Church roll list, a Spanish coin dated 1772, and the names of the Building Committee: John R. Wilson, John A. Bryson, John S. Junk, Miss S. E. Baird, and J. L. Malcolm. There were other miscellaneous items, as well.

Later that spring, the session received a letter from Mrs. Josephine M. Miller, daughter of the late Edgar J. Frost, requesting the Bible that had been removed from the cornerstone. (These names have been changed for privacy.) She said it was placed there by her father and designated by him to be given to a descendant. The session granted her request and sent her the Bible. Once all valuable objects were removed from the Church Street building and brought to Trinity, the "claiming" began. For the many years to come, "Firsts" and "Seconds" insisted constantly upon the items they "knew" were "theirs."

"These are *our* dishes."

"The lights in the chapel came from *Second* Church."

"The communion trays are from *First Church*."

Over time, many of these details have been lost. Since so much claiming was going on, no one remembers what unmarked heirlooms were for sure brought from the Second Church building. Only some silverware, dishes and a few objects specifically bear that name.

However, we do know that chimes were removed from the Second Presbyterian organ and installed in the new instrument of Trinity Church. These were re-dedicated in 1966 to the memory of those members of both former congregations who had given their lives in World War II. The organ itself was given to the Third Presbyterian Church of Uniontown. Finally, the church gifted the lovely "rose window" that had graced the Second Church sanctuary to the First Presbyterian Church in Inverness, Florida.

At the time of this writing, it has been a little over 50 years since the legendary union. Most Trinity Church members now say that the "First Church" and "Second Church" titles that were so long a regular part of Trinity culture have not been used for some time. Mary Martha, on the other hand, said that it still goes on.

"First Pres and Second Pres, sure," she said.

However, although "Firsts" and "Seconds" could see their differences clearly, they were not as obvious to the community around them.

A Trinity member who joined the church over 30 years after the merger has said, "One woman was a Second Church and showed me their dishes. 'This is *our* china,' she said. I was surprised. I had thought she was more of the First Church type!"

Trinity was still the church home of many of Uniontown's social elite. Perhaps without anyone realizing it, the First Church reputation was now being passed on to Trinity Church. Many parishioners were members of not just the church, but also the local Country Club. No one quite recalls when the church received its nickname, but it began to be called, "The Country Club Church," or just "The Country Club." First Church may have even been called this long before Trinity Church came into existence.

It seemed to Uniontown residents that the people of Trinity were all the "First Church" type. Whether members of the congregation minded or not, they could not avoid the common opinion. They would spend over 20 of the next years holding their unofficial title before finally, slowly, beginning to shake free of it.

During that time of great changes, the nation also transitioned with Trinity into a radically different era. The president was suddenly assassinated in 1963. During that same year, over 200,000 people marched on Washington to hear Martin Luther King Jr.'s "I Have a Dream" speech at the Lincoln Memorial. The country began to see dramatic sacrifices and strides for civil rights.

Yes, the days of bouffant hairdos and flat tops were ending. The next few years would usher in long hair and beards, blue jeans, t-shirts, wire-frames and sandals. There was a sense, perhaps, that nothing would ever be the same again.

However, although it had taken many years to adjust, First and Second Church members eventually did become Trinity Church.

"First and Second became good friends and merged, but it took a while," said Mary Martha.

As the parishioners had moved forward under incredibly tense circumstances, their strengthening hearts at last combined, and they became a church family who flowed onward together like a stream. As water finding its way through and around obstacles, they faced hardships together. They cried together, laughed together and ministered together. Whether it had been their choice to unite or not, what was once a divided house had transformed into a unified home.

In April 1979, Dr. Ross, in speaking of the future, told a Tribune Review journalist, "Our prayer is that our congregation ever increases in its worship and work, and that the witness of its members be evident throughout the community – and even beyond."

This writer in particular believes that as a defiant watercourse that has fought its way resiliently down from a rocky mountain top in order to nourish the life around it, this story, too, ultimately became a testimony to the glory of the One who directed its path. I would say their prayer was answered.

What about you?

That They All May Be One

Top: Rev. Dr. Vincent T. Ross
Bottom: The Second Presbyterian Church building

Trinity Church Tales to Remember

The sanctuary and chancel area of the Second Presbyterian Church building

the road from port charlotte

'Twas grace that taught my heart to fear, An∢ grace my fears reliev'∢;
How precious ∢i∢ that grace appear The hour I first believ'∢!

John Newton (1725–1807)

L ITERALLY THOUSANDS OF FAYETTE COUNTY RESIDENTS HAVE UTILIZED THE SERVICES OF INTERFAITH VOLUNTEER CAREGIVERS OF FAYETTE THROUGH THE YEARS. At the time of this writing, the not-for-profit organization has for over two decades provided outreach to older adults living in their own homes. The helpful services include transportation to medical appointments, visitation, grocery shopping, respite, minor home repairs, referrals, and much more. These services are all free of charge and provided with no income guidelines. The goal of Interfaith is only to help aging persons who live alone to do so with as much dignity and independence as possible.

Who provides the services? Interfaith has a network of volunteers from all over the community, primarily from the churches. The volunteers and those who donate to the mission in other ways are as diverse as the group they assist.

Many Uniontown residents know about Interfaith, but most have never heard the extraordinary story of how it came into being. Those who were around for the birth of the project will tell you that it has never been spearheaded by anyone with a human mind. No, they would say, Interfaith was always meant to be, and hardly anyone can disagree that the unique circumstances surrounding it were carried out supernaturally.

When the ministry was first established in the early 1990s, numerous faith stories emerged with it. Many Trinity Church members were involved with the program from its infancy, and they are the ones who still bear witness to countless strange and wonderful events. If you want to know more, simply ask them.

They would be happy to tell you. Each of their incredible stories is worthy of its own place in this volume. Yet for our purposes, this writer has delved into just one. This is the experience of the person who still sits behind the executive director's desk in the quaint, original office where the mission first became a real organization. The talkative, bright-eyed, gray-haired administrator looked me in the eyes and spoke so sincerely that anyone else listening would have believed every word she said, too.

Her name is Carol Ashton, and she has been a member of Trinity Church since 1998. The thriving, multi-church organization that she now directs traces its humble roots back to Trinity. Parishioners there started the program in 1991 as a pilot project called Senior Ministries. Carol was first hired at that time as the Volunteer Coordinator.

This is her story.

In the late fall of 1985, Carol was in Okeechobee, Florida visiting her daughter Terri. She also had an old friend who resided in the state, and she had planned to visit her at some point as well. But as time ebbed away, Carol found herself resisting the meeting. Maybe she would make up an excuse for not going. Perhaps she would just tell her she did not have time? Maybe on the next trip, she would say.

You see, Jeanne Vargo had become "religious." The once Harley Davidson-driving, thrill-seeking, 45-year-old Carol knew that the two of them would not have any fun now, especially if her friend refused to even go out for drinks.

More time passed. Carol still resisted. *Don't go, ₫on't go,* the voice inside her head insisted, and she agreed.

With only a few days left, Carol started to think of the good relationship she and Jeanne once shared. Reluctantly, she decided she had better visit.

The woman lived in Port Charlotte. The only way to get there from Okeechobee was to cross what locals had come to call Alligator Alley. It was a long, lonely, two-lane stretch that cut over to the coast.

As Carol was driving the little 5-speed she had borrowed from her daughter, she began to pass abandoned, boarded up buildings strewn haphazardly along the silent way. She realized she had not seen any people for some time and understood only too late that she would be in trouble if she happened to break down.

The Road from Port Charlotte

To her relief, civilization soon began to appear. She came into the area where her friend lived, but in her search for a street called Ivanhoe, she discovered there were two. After a few aimless circles, she at last pulled into Jeanne's driveway only to discover that she had a flat tire. The shiny nail head poking up out of the rubber seemed to say, "Well, I tried to stop you back there, but I guess now you have to stay."

Carol ended up visiting with Jeanne for days, rehashing fond memories, making new ones and eventually replacing the tire. But just as she suspected, it did not take long for the nagging to start.

"I want you to go to church with me on Sunday," her friend would say.

"Nah, I think I'll go back on Saturday," Carol would reply.

"Oh, please stay and go to church," Jeanne begged.

To be polite, Carol finally consented. *But*, she thought, *don't ask me to go up front because I'm not doing that.*

The church service was regular at first. Carol had been a member of the Central Christian Church back home in Uniontown for many years with her husband's family. Before that, she had gone to a Methodist church. She knew what church services were like. That's why she noticed right away when something started to not feel right.

The pastor, Carol realized, seemed to have written his sermon just for her. How could that be? His words seemed to slice through her heart like slivers of lightning and quicken it to life in a way she had never experienced before. She could hardly believe the feeling. The draw was overwhelming.

Tears welled in her eyes as she sat quietly hoping no one would notice. Gradually, she knew what she had to do. It was what she needed and wanted to do. At the pastor's suggestion, she silently asked Jesus Christ to come into her heart.

"But," she told Jesus, "I'm not going up front. You have to get me from here."

At her invitation, the Lord took up residence in her life that very moment, and something seemed to explode like a firework inside her heart as He did.

When the church service was over, Carol told Jeanne goodbye, but she did not share her news. It was too new and wild, and she was not sure what to say.

As she drove back across the long stretch from Port Charlotte, a deep peace suddenly began to fall down over her like a sheet until it fully enveloped and filled her. It was as nothing she had ever known before. She suddenly thought, *I'm going to heaven when I die*, and in an instant, she realized that all fear of death had left her. She would soon be taking a plane home to Pennsylvania, and if the aircraft happened to come crashing down, she would be okay.

She thought of the old song she had sung so many times, Amazing Grace. How precious the grace of God did appear in that magical hour following her belief. To this day, tears still come to her eyes every time she remembers the line.

Later, Carol could not even recall the words of the sermon that morning, but she knew her life would never be the same.

First, when she returned to Uniontown, Carol found she could no longer stay at her job in a restaurant. The language of some of the youthful employees and their general unwillingness to practice faith suddenly became disheartening. Although she had just purchased a new car, she told her husband, "I can't work there," and suddenly quit.

Don Ashton had noticed his wife was different. She still had not told anyone about her radical decision, but she could not hide it. She even stopped socializing with their friends whose values and views on faith were now even more different than her own. The atmosphere no longer felt right.

The only person she did tell was the pastor of the church in Port Charlotte. She had not been home long before she wrote a letter to him explaining how much his sermon had meant to her and that she had been "born again." Little did she know, Jeanne was also writing a letter to him telling him how her friend Carol was suffering and in need of prayer. The surprised pastor received both letters at the same time.

Meanwhile, Carol was not unemployed long before a job opportunity opened at the Community Action Agency in Uniontown. The position was for a supervisor for the homebound meals program. Although Carol's heart had been steering toward social work, she almost did not accept when it was offered to her. She had started to feel uneasy working with food again. However, in the middle of turning the job down, she recalled recent prayers to God asking Him for a position with good hours that allowed her to attend church. She was shocked and delighted to find her personal relationship with God was growing and that He kept coming through for her. She changed her mind and accepted the job.

In the Community Action kitchen, Carol began to prepare 300 meals daily with no volunteer assistance to help her. She soon recruited a few volunteers herself to ease the load. Over time, Carol eventually moved downstairs to an office position connecting clients to the services they needed. She was helping people, and she felt that was exactly where she wanted to be. That is – until a friend who also worked in the same building brought her an application for a new grant-funded program at his church.

For a whole year, members of Trinity United Presbyterian Church of Uniontown under the direction of their pastor, the Reverend Dr. John Sharp, had been assessing the greatest needs of the Uniontown community. Dr. Sharp had encouraged the fellowship to look at the changes in their neighborhood. In the past, people would walk to church and congregations had been brimming with families and children. Now the Uniontown population and their needs were different. Dr. Sharp felt it was time for the churches to respond.

He began to ask Trinity members some questions. How does a downtown church begin to represent the fellowship of Christ? How were they going to be of service and fulfill that sense of discipleship? Most importantly, what did they need to do to be faithful to Christ?

A planning group began to meet together each month to gather information about the community and to take a look at what Trinity's strengths were as a church. They did demographic studies and conversed with others in the county as well. What they soon discovered was that many elderly residents were alone and unable to travel. They could not make repairs or even keep their cupboards stocked. Even worse, they were desperately lonely. Many who had once been active church members were now homebound and alienated from their congregations.

At the time, local newspapers reported that 23.8 percent of Fayette County's population was over the age of 60. According to Carol, Southwestern Pennsylvania is still said to have the second largest population of elderly in the United States today.

It began to be clear to Dr. Sharp and the planning committee that God was leading them to minister to the elderly residents of their neighborhood. Now they had a focus. They set to work putting the pieces into motion for what they would call the Senior Ministries Program.

The committee decided that the new ministry would be under the direction of an area clergy member. They would also hire a Volunteer Coordinator. The coordinator would be responsible for going into the several high-rise apartment buildings near the church to interview the seniors living there. He or she would then assign healthy, able-bodied, volunteer retirees to respond to the various needs.

Soon, the church was granted initial funding from the Redstone Presbytery of the PC(USA) that would last for three years. Now they could hire their staff.

When it came to the volunteer coordinator position, Trinity Church member John Rapano thought of Carol Ashton. He had known her for some time and believed she could do a good job helping to develop the new program. He hand-delivered the application to her.

Carol had been working at Community Action for five years by then, but as she thought and prayed about the position at Trinity her heart seemed to sing. She imagined doing the work, and the pull was unmistakable. Ever since she had asked Jesus into her life, she was learning how to follow God. This was what He wanted her to do, she was sure of it. She wasted no time in applying and was ecstatic when the church called her to meet with them. The lively, blue-eyed blonde bounced into the interview room at Trinity Church all smiles and glowing.

Afterward, she waited. Days passed. Finally, unable to stand it any longer, she called the Reverend Dr. John Sharp on a Tuesday to inquire of the status. He gave her the devastating news. They had hired someone else. Her hopes sank to the ground.

"The only reason being that you didn't have your degree completed," Dr. Sharp told her gently.

The next day, Carol went to work with the pieces of her broken heart taped together. She had been so certain that job was where God wanted her to go next that she was shocked and wounded. She took a deep breath and said to herself, "Well, I had better rededicate myself to this agency."

However, she only had one day to mourn her loss. On Thursday, Dr. Sharp called back. "Carol, there has been a mistake," he said. He proceeded to ask her if she could come back in for a second interview.

Carol was so stunned that she could not even answer at first. When she found her voice, she told him she could.

The Road from Port Charlotte

The second interview was more intimidating than the first. Carol walked into a room with five prominent men of the church to include Paul Williams, Judge Edward Dumbauld, and Hugh Barclay. Mr. Barclay was the former Director of the Uniontown Center of Waynesburg College and now the CEO of the Pennsylvania State University Fayette Campus.

Carol glanced at Mr. Barclay. *School's out,* she thought. *I hope he doesn't remember me as a student because that will not be good.*

When she was seated, the questioning began. The search committee had prepared possible scenarios and wanted to know how Carol would respond to each one.

"Carol," one of the sturdy, serious, and well-dressed men began, "what would you do if somebody was dying and they wanted to take their life? How would you handle it?"

True to her nature, Carol said the first thing that popped into her mind. She smiled. "Well, I don't know how I would handle it, but I'm sure I could do it."

She later shook her head thinking of her responses. She was certain the only reason they hired her that day was because they did not have any choices left. Whatever had happened to the first person, it was a miracle she had the job.

"If it makes you feel better," Dr. Sharp encouraged her later, "I was also their second choice."

Knowing she was not first choice, Carol knew she had to prove herself. The only problem was, she had no idea what to do. She sometimes wondered why she was not more afraid, but she held on to her faith. "Well," she would say to herself, "Jesus did not bring me here to fail."

Indeed, friends and mentors began to surround her. Many would stand by her side for the next several years.

One day, Hugh Barclay himself made his way up to her office. It was on the second floor in the church building above the church office and overlooking the wide-open chapel below. Carol would often laugh thinking that she had always wanted a "lofty" job. When Hugh rounded the corner that day, she looked up, surprised.

"Carol, I'm dedicated to making this program work," he said. "And I'm dedicated to making you succeed."

According to Carol, Hugh was very strong in his faith. She found him to be a kind and compassionate man with a sense of humor. True to his word, he would follow her until the dream of Senior Ministries was fully realized.

In the beginning, Carol's first task was to go into the high-rise apartment buildings to do a spiritual survey of the elderly residents. At first, the managers of the buildings were leery.

"Why would a church want to come in here? We don't have any problems. We handle everything." – she was told.

One manager finally hesitated. "Well," he said slowly, "we do have this one woman in one of the apartments. She hasn't changed her clothes in three weeks..."

"Have you called mental health services?" Carol asked.

As it turned out, the manager knew nothing about the services offered in the community and Carol was suddenly allowed to enter the building.

Although the apartment residents were also reluctant to talk to her at first, once Carol was inside their homes, she had trouble leaving. Neither the residents nor Carol could have expected just how lonely and starved for conversation they were. Carol could barely make it to her other appointments on time each day because she was continually held up at the one previous.

Once the surveys were completed, Carol began addressing the needs. She and Trinity volunteers took care of medical transportation, visitation, grocery shopping and minor home repairs. They even had an 85-year-old electrician who volunteered to do electrical work as needed.

Soon, calls were coming in from all over town. The mission spread as volunteers were requested beyond the apartment buildings. Many elderly living on their own in Uniontown had families outside the area. Now larger volunteer projects began to take place, such as the building of ramps for confined persons.

Although some of the homes Carol had to visit from time to time were challenging situations with very disturbed individuals, she was never afraid. She chalked it up to having been sent, and God had equipped her with the skills she needed. "I really like going with you because I can be myself," a shy, aged woman said to her one day on their way to a medical appointment.

Carol's stories began to accumulate. Stories of grief and sadness, stories of hope, stories of joy and laughter. And some stories too fun not to share. Even

The Road from Port Charlotte

Dr. Sharp could hardly believe the accounts Carol told during coffee break each morning.

Once, a well-dressed German woman who spoke with broken English had been requesting rides to visit her boyfriend, who was 90 years old. When he passed away, Carol never heard his name mentioned again. Instead, the woman asked, "Do you have any other men?"

Soon, there was no denying that between counseling and coordinating, Carol and the volunteers were quite busy. The need was severe, and the program was working. In their first year, Senior Ministries had made more than 400 home visits alone to the elderly. Reinforcements were needed.

Carol had imagined that the other Presbyterian churches would be the first to help. Instead, she was surprised to receive a phone call one day from a sweet, young Catholic nun.

"I would like to go with you on visits," said Sister Elaina.

That was more than alright with Carol. Within no time, the new helper began making phone calls herself and taking on other responsibilities as well.

Soon enough, Carol heard from a very concerned Catholic daughter of one of the clients.

"Carol, you had better come and re-evaluate my mother because she has slipped over the edge," she said.

"What makes you think that?"

"She told me a Presbyterian Church sent a Catholic nun to come visit."

Carol laughed. "There's nothing wrong with your mother."

Already, the ministry was beginning to draw in volunteers from across the churches and denominations, and it would not stop. Volunteers started coming in from everywhere.

At the end of three years, all who were involved in Senior Ministries knew that the program had become much bigger than they had ever envisioned. It seemed to grow without any effort at all. Demand rose constantly, and the volunteers poured in as though someone had sent them at just the right time. At one point, there were almost a few hundred volunteers serving several hundred individuals.

"It was phenomenal," said Dr. Sharp once when remembering back. "Everyone steps back and looks at it and says, 'This isn't something we did.' We were guided, clearly. We weren't smart enough to figure this all out the way it came together."

As the requests for help kept coming from throughout the county, it was evident that the ministry needed to become an organization of its own.

During that time, Rabbi Sion David, the spiritual leader of Temple Israel in Uniontown, was the executive director of the program. He acted as the liaison between the Uniontown clergy and Senior Ministries. Rabbi David discovered an international organization called Interfaith Volunteer Caregivers, and the new name was agreed upon. The formation of the organization in Uniontown occurred in 1993.

"Can you believe this?" Dr. Sharp asked Carol at that time.

Speaking off the cuff as always, she replied, "This must have been a real test of faith for you."

She felt like slapping her hand over her mouth, but he just softly replied, "Yes."

Dr. Sharp was a humble man. He was a deep thinker and very patient. The secretary at Trinity Church during his pastorate has claimed that he was always down to earth with everyone no matter who they were. He treated every person equal and with respect. She said that just about everyone who remembers him as pastor would agree, and though it's difficult to please all, no one can remember anyone in the congregation at that time who did not feel the same way. Dr. Sharp was "one of them." He never preferred the title "Dr." He was always just John, and when he was around there was always laughter.

In fact, upon being offered the job at Trinity, Carol's aunt had told her Presbyterians were "stiff," and she was not going to have any fun. As irony would have it, Carol had never laughed so much as when she worked with the staff at Trinity Church.

But Interfaith could no longer stay based at Trinity Church. Their office would have to be moved in order to send the message that this was not just one church. This organization was an opportunity for all churches to be involved.

In February 1994, more grants awarded to Trinity on behalf of Interfaith were used to establish an office in Suite 106 at the Community Service Building on Beeson Avenue. Interfaith is still located there at the time of this writing.

The Road from Port Charlotte

In the meantime, Carol finished her degree in social work and became the executive director of the organization when Rabbi David resigned in the summer of 1996. Now the recruiting of volunteers from the churches was up to her. Most often, she would ask permission to present her message during Sunday morning services. When she did, congregations were nearly always left in tears.

From the start, Carol felt her responsibility when speaking with fellow brothers and sisters in Christ was to make them consider where their God-given gifts fit into the mission field of Fayette County. She did this by telling the real stories that she had gathered throughout the years.

"One man called the church once," she often would begin. "He had seen the article in the newspaper. He told me, 'Carol, I'm interested in that telephone reassurance thing you do. I want you to call every morning, but I don't want to talk to you. I just want you to call so I know I didn't die in the middle of the night.'"

At this point, she would let the giggles ripple across the crowd and then die off before she went on. She alone could see the few heads nodding. Those elderly parishioners who lived alone knew all too well the fear of passing away with no one knowing it.

"This is the great fear," she would say. "There was a man who died in New Salem. He was actually dead for three weeks before anyone found him because no one was checking on him."

Now there was always silence. She had their attention, and she was on her way to having their hearts.

"I support foreign missions," she would say. "The mission field is across the world. Across the nation. But more often than not, it's across the street. It's all around us. We drive up and down our streets and don't know who our neighbors are. The whole concept of Interfaith is neighbor helping neighbor. There is a real mission field right here in Fayette County."

Carol hoped the shocking stories would cause her hearers to see the true need. One thing she had learned was that unless someone was a minister or a social worker, they rarely saw the homeless, hungry or destitute right before their eyes. However, as Jesus told his disciples, the poor would always be among us.

"Just where are these people?" asked one well-dressed Trinity Church parishioner one Sunday as a group of women stood speaking with Carol.

"As a matter of fact, there was one I just 302'd from the porch of Trinity House this morning," she answered.

Carol had spotted the elderly woman more than once hiding among trash bags and bushes in the shadows of the old manse. Each time the woman saw Carol approach, she quickly scuttled away. It was becoming very cold outside, and Carol was eventually able to reach out. The woman received the help she needed at a mental health institution. This was all unbeknownst to the church members until that afternoon.

The poverty-stricken were not always the only ones who the volunteers and local church members alike were surprised to meet through Interfaith. Carol had rarely come in contact with racial prejudice prior to then, but since working for the organization, she was faced with the reality often.

Since Carol had grown up walking to school in a predominantly African American community, this was new for her. She quickly came to believe that any type of racial prejudice was learned in the home.

Although the country had made legislative headway with the Civil Rights Act of 1964, some people seemed to cling to the ways of thinking with which they had grown up. Even today, Sunday morning has still been said to be one of the most segregated times of the week.

Yet, Christ-like efforts stemmed by Interfaith began to chip away at the ingrained thinking of some who still adhered to it in Uniontown at the time.

An aging woman one day called Carol to request visitation on a regular basis. Carol knew the perfect volunteer. Though, so that it would not come as a surprise, she carefully let the client know that the volunteer was married to a black man.

"Oh, well, I can't have her in my house. I have good dishes," - was the response.

Carol assured the woman that the volunteer would not steal from her and that she had already taken care of many others in the church. After some persuading, the woman finally agreed to let the volunteer come.

Remarkably, a deep friendship blossomed between the two. The volunteer's husband shoveled the snow in the winter and helped with other yard work and repairs. The volunteer herself did more than she had been required and visited much more often as well.

Just before passing away, the client, who had a changed heart, said to Carol, "To think that I almost let prejudice get in the way of somebody really helping me."

Ten years after Carol began to work with Interfaith, she and Don Ashton decided to join Trinity Church. Until then, they had kept their membership at Central Christian and attended both churches back and forth.

Today, Interfaith is a sub-contracting agency of the Southwestern Pennsylvania Human Services Area Agency on Aging, and they receive additional funding and support from individuals, corporations, service clubs, churches and private foundations. The organization has always been a good avenue for relationships across the various churches and denominations, churches that that normally would not even communicate with one another.

Dr. Sharp said later that he and Trinity Church members need to remind themselves sometimes that Interfaith happened because people got together and were serious about their faith. They were willing to let God lead instead of thinking they had the answers. He said the planning meetings for the first year were rather boring, and the committee members often wondered if they really knew what they were doing and if they truly thought the idea would work. To the surprise of them all, it did.

"Of all the times that I left the house to go to 'just another meeting' wondering if it was going to amount to anything, these were the meetings that became something truly amazing," he said.

According to Dr. Sharp, Trinity Church members were faithful in believing that what they needed to do was reach out, and that God would make it work. Thousands of people in the community have benefited from that faith.

Carol has said that she never planned on being the executive director of a not-for-profit organization which she helped to develop from the ground up. It was not a prospect for her wildest dreams. Even now when she goes out into the community to minister, she still prays no one recognizes her from the Harley Davidson days. What always encourages her to move forward is to look back and know that what was accomplished has never been her doing. She was merely a willing worker whom God chose and prepared to do His will where He placed her. Indeed, it was truly He who put every piece into place for the organization. Carol, Trinity Church, and the rest of the team of past and present have simply been fortunate enough to go along for the ride and tell about it.

Many trying circumstances have since plagued Carol and her family through the years. A life working in the ministry is rarely without its troubles, and that is not to mention the personal trials. Carol's faith at times has become weakened when a battle rages for her mind. She sometimes thinks that the devil might win, like he almost did in preventing her from visiting Jeanne Vargo years ago. However, she need simply recall the moment on the road from Port Charlotte. The moment when she knew she was saved.

The moment of belief in Jesus, as the old song indicates, is a sacred one in each Christian's story. It is when a sinner has stopped walking down one road and has turned to embark on quite another adventure, one worth every risk and filled with untold blessings from the Father of Lights.

Wherever you find yourself on the road of life, Carol would have you know that if you have entrusted your steps to Jesus as Savior and Lord, you will never walk in darkness. His hand will lead you to exactly where you need to be, every time.

We have now come to the end of this story. Few people today know that Interfaith Volunteer Caregivers of Fayette was started in a small room of Trinity Church and maintained in those days by dedicated Trinity volunteers. Now you, dear reader, do. Fewer still may believe that it was breathed to life by a source not of this world, but that is exactly what Carol and her Trinity counterparts would tell you.

What do you think?

Sources

Newspapers:

"Trinity's Program reaches out to community elderly." *Herald-Standard* [Uniontown] 1 May 1992: n.p. Print.

Borsodi Zajac, Frances. "IVCF: Volunteer Group Serves Area's Elderly and Disabled." *Herald-Standard* [Uniontown] 22 July 1994: C6. Print.

Borsodi Zajac, Frances. "Ashton New Leader of Interfaith Volunteer Caregivers." *Herald-Standard* [Uniontown] 8 Nov. 1996: C6. Print.

Kroeger, Judy. "Faith In Action." *The Daily Courier*. Celebrate Life's Journey insert [Connellsville] 20 Nov. 1999: 6. Print.

Personal Interviews:

Carol Ashton, church member and Executive Director of Interfaith Volunteer Caregivers of Fayette

Rev. Dr. John Sharp, Pastor Emeritus of Trinity United Presbyterian Church, Uniontown

John Rapano, church member

Note: In 2019, Interfaith Volunteer Caregivers of Fayette County came full circle and relocated their office back to Trinity Church. The office on Beeson Avenue had suffered flooding from nearby Redstone Creek, and there was the possibility of it happening again.

Top: Carol Ashton as Senior Ministries Volunteer Coordinator in 1991
Bottom: Don and Carol Ashton with their friends Jeanne and Frank Vargo

a narrow escape

I F YOU LOOK AT TRINITY CHURCH, it is easy to believe that the fortress will stand forever. Like the ruins of ancient Rome, everything else may be gone, but a grand structure such as this one will remain.

That is why church secretary Linda Chidester was shocked on the evening of Thursday, July 27, 2000. The church sexton had just called at 9:30 to give her some of the most chilling news she had ever received concerning the church building. Stone blocks from high above had come crashing down.

Linda rushed to the scene where police had roped off the area with caution tape. She could hardly believe what she saw. An ornate cornerstone from the sanctuary roof above had fallen and broken in half in the grassy flowerbed at the base of the concrete steps of the center porch. One of the pieces had rolled out onto the sidewalk. It alone weighed about a ton, she later found out. Three large sandstone slabs had also flown down after as a result. Two of them speared the landing of the concrete stairs below, and the third had soared through the air even farther to land in the vines on the other side of the stairs.

The most important question was, why had it happened? After a century, was Uniontown finally in danger of worn mortar and raining sandstone from Trinity Church?

As Linda looked up at the gaping hole in the roof that was black and shadowed by the night sky, she shivered. The remaining three slaps were still in place, for now, but they had shifted eerily as though threatening to also come thundering down with the slightest breath.

The crushed porch was located right outside of the church office. For as long as Linda could recall, someone was nearly always walking along the Morgantown Street sidewalk outside the office window, day or night. Walkers often even stopped to take a rest on the porch stairs. Church members also used the porch as it led to a secondary entrance of the sanctuary. As Linda made her way home, she could not help but think that if someone had been there when the stones fell, they would not have survived. By the grace of God, no one had been there. Trinity Church members thanked the Lord for that.

As time went on, even more evidence of the Almighty's sovereign hand came into the minds of Linda and others. To begin with, not only had no one been in harm's way, but no one had even seen the stones fall. An employee of a nearby gas station had happened to notice the destruction and informed the authorities. When the police arrived, not a soul was there to meet them. It was they who contacted the sexton in the first place. Next, only one piece of stone had come to rest on the sidewalk. All four of the others had landed on Trinity property. Not one solid piece of masonry had smashed into the street only a mere few feet away.

The next morning, a man named Wendell Charles of Hopwood Enterprises was investigating the property across Morgantown Street from the church. He had been hired to work on another project for Trinity. The site where he stood would soon be a new church parking lot once the former WMBS radio building there was demolished. Although the Rev. Dr. Sharp and his family were on vacation, the congregation did not hesitate to act. They requested Wendell's aid. Thankfully, he was available to take on the emergency project.

Wendell's crews began the long process of clearing the fallen stone away from the sidewalk and drilling pins to secure the unsteady slabs above as a temporary measure until a permanent solution could be put into place.

For the first step toward getting the permanent repairs underway, church member Paul Wood quickly made contact with Altman & Altman Architects in Uniontown. Their office mailed a proposal request to four masonry restoration contractors. Of these, Mariani & Richards, Inc. of Pittsburgh was selected to do the job.

The contractor agreed to reset the fallen copingstones into their original positions on the north gable with new mortar. The stones would be secured to the wall with stainless steel dowels. The porch and stairs would also be repaired.

While the work was taking place, the mystery of the fallen stones came to light. It was concluded that vibrations from vehicles passing by, including the heavy brakes of the big rigs and the loud speaker systems of cars and trucks, had shaken the building through the years. The corner piece had come loose and was finally pushed out of place by the slabs leaning heavily against it.

Now, Trinity's congregation began to identify other needs for long-term durability of the structure. It might cause the reader to wonder if perhaps the sudden catastrophe was actually a divine wakeup call alerting the congregation to do just that. The shocking incident did serve as the catalyst that encouraged many more building repairs. The church members dutifully arose to better vigilance so that something worse would not happen.

The next big project on the church building became to repoint the exterior, especially in the most fragile areas. Additional physical deterioration and damage had already been addressed during the Reverend Dr. Sharp's pastorate. Even the Tiffany stained-glass windows had been sent off a few at a time to be cleaned. Additional braces were also added to them. Further renovations occurred when the Reverend Michael Orsted came to the church as the next pastor. These projects included some interior updates in the sanctuary.

The series of church building repairs culminated in the fall of 2004 with an exterior cleaning. For the first time in its history, years of pollution and grime were removed from Trinity Church. This elaborate project was a gift from Fayette County Commissioner Joseph A. Hardy III. He had added the undertaking to a list of many other downtown revitalization jobs in preparation for the Professional Golfers' Association of America tournament that would soon be held in nearby Nemacolin Woodlands Resort. Thousands of people would travel through Uniontown as a result of the event.

The cleaning work was done by the Raimondo Painting, Cleaning and Wall Repair Co. of Greensburg. They restored the church building to its original color, which no current Uniontown resident had ever known. Their efforts also better revealed the intricate details of the stonework on the gable peaks, columns, arches and entryways.

On October 17, 2004, the Trinity congregation rededicated their building to the service of God, and they thanked Mr. Hardy for his donation.

Since those years of extensive repair work, even more alarming roof damage was discovered. Leaks from the tallest rooftops had been allowing water to trickle down into the sanctuary from above. This was believed to have been happening for quite some time. The water loosened the plaster around the cherub faces and intricate designs near the sanctuary ceiling. Flakes of plaster with hints of gold paint started to drop to the floor below. At the time of this writing, the problem has not yet been fully resolved. Although the high roof has been repaired, the plaster damage in the sanctuary is now another issue.

Although repair work to the building can be found in the session minutes spanning the whole life of the structure, the once glorious monument is finally, truly showing signs of its age. With church attendance dropping the same as many other downtown, traditional churches across America, the funds available to care for the great edifice will perhaps one day be no more.

What will become of Trinity Church? The reflections of some who have loved her are contained in the next story of this volume.

Sources

Newspapers:

Zalar, Amy. "Watch Out Below: Stones Topple from 104-Year-Old Fayette Street Church." *Herald Standard* [Uniontown] n.d.: n.p. Print.

"City Congregation to Rededicate Church." *Herald Standard* 15 Oct. 2004: n.p. heraldstandard.com. Web. 1 July 2015.

Church Records:

Building and Grounds Files

Personal Interview:

Linda Chidester, former church member and former Church Secretary of Trinity United Presbyterian Church, Uniontown

A Narrow Escape

When stones fell off the roof — July 2000.

chronicle of a legacy

WHEN INFORMATION IS STILL COMMON KNOWLEDGE, there does not seem to be anything special about it. Yet as time ebbs away, memories, stories and facts increase in their value.

Long ago, many of the early records of the Presbyterian Church in Uniontown were not multiplied or printed. Though the lost information is believed to have been meager, surely it would have been meaningful to us today.

Trinity Church members are grateful for the history that was preserved, much of which has been used to write this small book. Undoubtedly, the tales documented here will also continue to grow more important as the years press on. These accounts and the ones yet to be written will serve future generations of Uniontown in remembering their ecclesiastical history. The story of Trinity Church is important not just for church members, but also for the entire community.

In the spirit of contributing to the preservation effort, this final Trinity tale has been recorded. The story you now read is the stirring chronicle of one of the oldest church fellowships of Uniontown. A legacy of rich history and dauntless faith is being passed on to Trinity successors.

It begins nearly 250 years before this writing...

In the spring of 1768, the man to be credited with founding Uniontown, Henry Beeson, left his homeland of Virginia for a long journey. He and his wife and their infant son set out north with a plan to ultimately settle on property that Henry owned at the Great Falls, later to be known as Louisville, Kentucky. But they had one special stop to make first.

The Beesons were on their way to visit an old friend who had settled in a valley country encircled by the densely-forested mountains of the Pennsylvania colony. Henry was 25 years old at the time, and he had heard about the wild frontier lands where his former neighbor, Thomas Gist, now resided. Thomas had wanted Henry to come and settle in the region with him. The first parts of this area being settled at the time are now known as the counties of Washington, Fayette, Westmoreland and Allegheny, as well as the areas along the Monongahela and Ohio Rivers.

Despite Thomas' coaxing, Henry was not persuaded. That is, until he approached the crest of a hill along Braddock's Road and beheld the view. The richly hued horizon lay to the west of the Gist settlement in the lush valley below. Another former neighbor, William Crawford, had also settled nearby. It is said that as Henry stood taking in the beauty around him, he decided that this was where he and his family were going to settle after all.

When the Beesons arrived at the home of Thomas and his sister Anne, their friends were overjoyed to hear that they planned to stay. Henry soon selected a piece of land despite warnings that the mere sight of white men could cause an "Indian uprising."

However, not long afterward, the natives in the area sold all of their remaining claims to the southwestern portion of Pennsylvania. Henry was able to make an application in the land office in Philadelphia for 255 acres on Redstone Creek, which he named Mount Vernon. He proceeded to build a one-and-a-half story log house at the present location of the Mount Vernon Towers apartment building in Uniontown. Prior to the apartment building, this location was also the site of the exquisite home of J.V. Thompson's niece, Lida Eleanor Nicolls, the Princess of Thurn and Taxis.

Many worrisome run-ins with natives did occur throughout the Beeson's stay in their new home, but Henry continued to expand his land holdings nonetheless. In the meantime, his brother Jacob also made the trip northward across the mountains to settle a mile west of the tiny village and his brother.

Before long, Henry purchased an additional 300 acres upon which he built a mill, attracting other settlers. Due to the occasional distress from natives, Henry also built a blockhouse in 1774. When trouble broke out, settlers could flee to the protection and safety of the stockade.

As the Beeson family continued to grow through the years, Henry constructed what became known as "Henry Beeson's Mansion." It was a large home located on present South Beeson Avenue.

Meanwhile, as more families continued to move into the area, Henry began to conceive the idea of laying out a town. On July 4, 1776, coincidentally the same day the Declaration of Independence of the United States of America was signed, Henry posted a notice for the Beeson's Town Lottery. Most of the 54 lots would be drawn 16 days later for the purpose of purchasing a property and constructing a dwelling on it.

When the day arrived, people came from many miles away to draw lots. It was so successful that Henry continued to buy land and divide it into lots for sale. His brother Jacob did the same. Henry named the settlement the Town of Union, but the villagers referred to their home as "Beeson's Town" or "Beesontown."

Later, Beesontown became the county seat after Fayette County broke from Westmoreland County in September 1783. Also, in 1787, Pennsylvania became a state.

All along, Henry and his wife had lived at the "mansion" raising their children and watching the village grow. It eventually became a borough under the name of Uniontown. Many business establishments were erected to include a potter, a hatter, a blacksmith, a silversmith, a tailor, a grocer and many more.

In 1804, it was time for a change for the Beesons. Henry and Mary moved a final time to Mt. Pleasant, Ohio, where they ended their days. Prior to leaving, Henry set aside a parcel of land deeded to the town inhabitants to be used as cemetery. Since the Methodists and the Baptists already had cemeteries, the land became known as the Presbyterian graveyard.

Members of the Presbyterian Church were later primarily buried in Oak Grove Cemetery, located along Route 40. Oak Grove was established in 1867 as the Union Cemetery of Fayette County. At that time, the remains of many people who were buried in other locations were moved to the site.

Though two had died, a number of Henry and Mary Beeson's 13 children had chosen to stay in the town after their parents left. Although Henry himself had been a Quaker, Beeson names begin appearing in the first pages of the Presbyterian Church of Uniontown register in the year 1825 with all indication that these individuals had already been members long before the Feb 24, 1825 official organization of the church.

The Beeson family has remained faithful to the church to present day at the time of this writing. In fact, Henry Beeson was the great, great, great, great grandfather of current Trinity Church member Pauline Semans, who is known as "Robin." It was through Robin's dedicated research that the information for the beginning part of the tale could be written. For a deeper look into the adventurous story of her ancestor, consult her book, *Beesontown: A Look Into the Past.*

Other names that appear at the start of the Presbyterian Church records include Campbell, Carroll, Ewing, Finley, Lewis and others. Some of these families were members of the church for many generations as well.

Two years prior to Henry Beeson's arrival in the region, the Reverends Charles Beatty and George Duffield had been sent by the Synod of Philadelphia to go with the Pennsylvania forces for the purpose of exploring the frontier settlements and assessing what could be done by way of missionary work among the natives. Others followed them.

The characteristics of the missionaries in those days were inspiring. They traveled on horseback or on foot without roads, bridges or ferries. Often, they would swim the creeks or rivers on Sabbath mornings just to preach in wet clothing and then rush away to other preaching appointments. They visited "waste places" to seek out "destitute people" and organize them into churches. Then they watched over the young fellowships until permanent pastors could be obtained. Despite all the dangers and hardships for missionaries and pioneer settlers alike, churches seemed to sprout up everywhere.

The Reverend Dr. James Power became the first minister to permanently remain in the Fayette County area. He was said to be tall and graceful with a "clear, methodical style" as an evangelical preacher. He was a graduate of Princeton and only 29 years old when he began his efforts in the region. Dr. Power arrived in 1774 to do missionary work and was eventually led to organize the Dunlap's Creek Presbyterian Church in Merritstown, which is the oldest organization west of the mountains, at least according to the recorded testimony of Dr. Power himself.

Dr. Power was also at times asked to preach to a small congregation that would soon enough become a powerful church in the region. Little is known about the early days of the Presbyterian congregation in Beesontown, but it had taken root by 1799, when the members requested supplies from the newly established Presbytery of Redstone. They fought the good fight with irregular preaching all the way to 1817, when they were finally able to secure their first permanent pastor.

The Reverend William T. Wylie from Washington County accepted the charge with a salary of $1,000, which was large for the time. Information passed down claims that he wore knee britches and shoes with silver buckles, and his hair was tied in a queue and powdered. Physically, he was imposing, standing over six feet tall with a slender build. He was pleasant to converse with and solemn in the pulpit. He is said to have preached without notes, and the flock regarded him as a powerful speaker. At the time, the congregation held their meetings in the local courthouse.

While living in Uniontown, Rev. Wylie built his own home, possibly located where the present Titlow Tavern, once a hotel, now stands. Tradition claims that his wife was responsible for having started the first Sunday School in the town with the help of a Miss Betsy Hadden. The meetings were held in the parsonage.

In those days, the church used tokens as a means to maintain the Lord's Table in a righteous manner. The small leaden chips were distributed by the minister or elders to church members who were deemed worthy of partaking communion. Only those with a token could participate in the sacrament. The long-held practice was abolished in 1830.

The first pastoral relationship with the Presbyterian Church came to an end in 1823 when Rev. Wylie left to go to Washington and Jefferson College. He returned later, probably to help care for the pastoral needs of the now shepherd-less flock.

Although the congregation that had grown steadily and substantially during Rev. Wylie's pastorate tried to call him as pastor again in 1827, he declined. For five long years, they struggled along in a discouraged state.

Beginning in 1825, the Presbyterian Church of Uniontown began sending reports to the Presbytery. They expressed their many sorrows, as death repeatedly knocked on their doors. They also spoke of despair regarding the "little evidence" of growing faith among their numbers. They knew they needed the Word of God preached to them, and they longed for consistency and spiritual leadership.

On April 7, 1827, elders Joseph Kibler and Thomas Lewis signed a report which stated:

> It will be seen by reference to the above report that little change has taken place in our branch of the church since our last report. Religion appears in a more gloomy state at present. Than for two or three years past, owing no doubt to divisions with respect to the settlement of a pastor: Society Meetings are still attended on the Sabbath, and the monthly concert: but not with so much apparent interest as we could

Chronicle of a Legacy

wish: Lukewarmness prevails with professions, generally, altho our sins abound, yet the mercies of God much more abound: Death has not been permitted to make his entrance within our little fold, since our last. We are still destitute of the States Ministrations of the Word and Ordinances of God. We not long since, moderated a call for a pastor (Rev. W. Wylie) and notified him of the fact, through our Moderator, but have not received an answer. Clouds and darkness surrounds us at present, but the Lord's will be done.

Many other reports reiterated the same sentiment. At last, in 1828, a Mr. John Holmes Agnew accepted a call to the little Presbyterian Church of Uniontown. With the leadership of a pastor, the congregation found solid footing and began to carry on their work in Uniontown.

The steady stream of well-respected, God-fearing ministers to follow Mr. Agnew continued to guide the church through days of both great hope and times of suffering. Over the decades, the congregation erected meeting houses as the need emerged, and they watched the town around them flourish and grow, just as they were finally growing spiritually. The record of these days and the biographical sketches of the ministers can be found in the *History of Redstone Presbytery*, 1889.

By the time the church was ready to erect the current edifice, the era of adventure and traveling into the unexplored and dangerous West had long ago ended. Uniontown was now a thriving town with a population of 10,000. Street cars and trains continuously carried shoppers and miners throughout the business district. These were the days of coal and coke - the next great age to impact the region.

After coal was mined, it was converted into coke in the area's beehive ovens and then shipped to Pittsburgh to be used for making steel. At the turn of the century, there were 28,000 beehive ovens in the county which lit the night sky with a fiery glow. Uniontown was said to have been surrounded by a "ring of fire" from the Oliver, Continental and Leith ovens.

The new industry brought money and people to Fayette County from far and wide. The county experienced a 52 percent increase in population from 1890 to 1900, and it would go up another 12 percent before 1920.

Nationally, this era was called the Gilded Age. Agriculture represented most of the economy until the Civil War in the early 1860s, but beginning with the railroads, industry had rapidly grown. Some small businesses were now large businesses, and by the end of the century, the nation's economy was dominated by a few, powerful individuals. Names such as John D. Rockefeller of Standard Oil, and Andrew Carnegie of Carnegie Steel were recognized across the country.

On Saturday, June 18, 1894, a crowd gathered to witness the cornerstone-laying ceremony for the new church building in Uniontown. Ministers of other denominations within the area were also present. Dr. Milholland, the pastor, had become ill and could therefore only remark briefly on the history of Presbyterians in Uniontown. Also, the Reverend Dr. Ralston, a former pastor who was expected to deliver the address, had also fallen ill and was not in attendance at all. In his stead, the message was given by the Reverend Dr. Boyle of the Methodist Episcopal Church, presently Asbury United Methodist.

Cornerstone Laying Ceremony
June 18, 1894

The audience listened to Dr. Boyle's words, and they loudly applauded when he finished.

"This ought to be an occasion of rare interest to all the churches," he said. "It indicates that the head of the church has highly favored you with temporal blessings, and that he has to munificently vouchsafed His spirit, that you have been moved to lay your substance upon His altar and unite in the erection of a building that will not only be adapted to religious services but that will be an expression of strength and symmetry that will be an educator for all who see it and all who worship within it. Your prosperity is our joy for your God is our God."

Dr. Boyle went on to say that this cornerstone laying ought also to be an occasion of rare interest to the community as well.

"The religious feature aside, the material advantage of this enterprise cannot be estimated. The building will not only be an ornament to the denomination that erects it, but it will be a substantial ornament to the town.

"I join my brethren of all the denominations represented on the platform in congratulating you upon the history not only of your local, but also of the great church with which you are identified. Its history of progress is seen in its educational institutions, its missionary enterprise, its halls of science and philosophy and its schools of literature. While it is keeping abreast of the times, it has been conservative enough not to obliterate the old land marks. It adheres to them today, not because they are old but because they are true. It's McMillans, its Marquises and its McCurdys preached the truth in righteousness over a century ago in Western Pennsylvania and they have been succeeded by a thoroughly educated ministry that has kept the faith of the fathers.

"As God has favored you so far in this undertaking, may He continue with you and spare you to enjoy this your Christian home."

Articles placed in the box for the cornerstone included: a copy of the Scriptures; names of the officers and members of the church; other lists of names from the various church societies; copies of each of the Uniontown newspapers and Presbyterian publications; programs; meeting minutes; and names of the architect, contractors and builders.

As the building went up in the years to follow, the town surely marveled.

In those days, the Young People's Christian Association that had started meeting at the First Presbyterian Church was "where the young men went to see their

girls home," according to a memory recorded in the church archives. Church was then a social center, and nearly everyone was affiliated with a local church.

After the erection of the magnificent structure, the nation continued to move forward in advancements. Uniontown adopted all the new updates to remain as relevant as possible. By 1906, Fayette County was at the height of the coal boom. There were 300 mines and 150 company-owned mining towns, called "patches," to house the workers. However, not everything in Uniontown could be great or glamorous during the boom time. A presence of crime also existed in the area which affected many.

Indeed, in the late 1800s, some of the most notorious outlaws of Fayette County were finally brought to justice. The Cooley Gang, as they were known, consisted of a group of armed men led by brothers Jack and Frank Cooley. Their hideout was hidden somewhere in the hills near Fairchance. They were mysterious in the sense that crimes were often blamed on them, but no one could know for sure. They also likely committed many crimes that remained concealed. By the end of 1892, their reign finally ended.

Injustice also prevailed on much higher levels as well. As individuals who were ruthless for power sometimes dominated the leading industries of the nation, corruption spread, and so did severe poverty. The presence of great wealth contrasted with the tremendous poverty that could be found all around it. Fifty years earlier, most Americans had worked for themselves, but by 1900, most worked for an employer. The relationship between wealthy employer and their dependent employees became strained. This concept shaped Fayette County and became a reality in the lives of those making a living at the time. It trickled down even into more recent times as well.

By 1914, the United States had become the largest industrial nation of the world. Several of Uniontown's residents had ascended to great fortunes. There were at least 13 millionaires before 1915, which was the most per capita of any city in the United States. Some of these were First Presbyterian Church members at the time of the building of the present structure.

Meanwhile, the population in the Uniontown area was surging. Immigrants came from Europe to provide the labor for the coal and coke industry. As they poured into the region, their many different nationalities and languages came with them, transforming the area for years to come.

"I had a member of a congregation who had children in a class where there were nine different languages," said Dr. John Sharp, Pastor Emeritus of Trinity Church. "There was Italian, Slovak and on and on. Can you imagine trying to teach a classroom of second graders?"

As the owners of the mines understood they held the monopoly on jobs, this became a problem for the residents of the little patch towns in Fayette County. Miners would often try to strike in order to be treated more fairly regarding wages and safety, but usually to no avail. In later years, labor would become more organized with the creation of unions. Until then, a constant battle for power existed.

Dr. Sharp remembers a piece of Uniontown history he once researched.

"The coal companies would charter a train to bring black workers to the mine," he said. "They were told when they were recruited in the south that they were going to break the strike of the miners. I remember being sympathetic to the idea of someone being brought here and sent down into a coal mine having no idea what they're supposed to do and how dangerous it was. It was the coal baron's effort to have control. In particularly, they were bringing untrained workers in simply to break the power of the European workers who were trying to strike because they felt they were being abused. This was a major display in the community of what the times were like."

Soon enough, the economic fortunes of Fayette County were dealt a severe blow by the bankruptcy of J. V. Thompson and the closing of his bank in 1915. It has been said that his ruin also ruined some of his friends, and it almost ruined Uniontown. Money no longer flowed through Fayette County as before, and the coal industry began to fade away. However, its shadow can still be seen on every street in the present city. Homes that were built during the Gilded Age still scatter downtown Uniontown. Streetcar and train tracks cut through the roads. Trinity Church and other structures erected with coal boom money are well-known fixtures in the county.

A class of the Second Presbyterian Church "prior to 1921" standing in front of their church building on Church Street.

First Row: Mr. Brehm (teacher), Mary Russell, Retta Bryson, Lizzie Allen, Rae Smith, Miss Kennedy, Rachel Hansel, Mrs. McCormick, Mr. Dunn

Second Row: Sadie Rankin, Miss Beatty, Mrs. Trax, Mrs. Chalfant, Mrs. Woodhall, Mrs. W.A. Rankin, Mrs. W.D. Rankin, Ora Dunn, Flora Williams, Adda Glenn, Mrs. Sproull, Cora Allen.

Third Row: Mrs. Moyer, Mrs. Hathaway, Mrs. Anna Summers, Mrs. Wise, Mrs. Jefferis

Fourth Row: Mrs. Behn, Jane Rankin, Allie Brey, Cora Bryson, Mrs. Joseph Norris, Mrs. Bowman, Mrs. Davidson, Pearl Watson

When the coal dust settled, residents picked themselves up as best as they could. At the First Presbyterian Church, the session met with the Board of Deacons to discuss "sittings in the church" in 1914. A committee was appointed for "arranging the congregation." This is the final indication of pew assignments. It is not known when the practice totally ceased.

After World War I, a John Ellsworth Hess is credited in the session minute books with donating a memorial plaque containing the names of those who had rendered service to their country. It is located on the wall of the front porch of the church building. John was the son of George W. and Mary Louise Hess, and the grandson of John and Amanda (Offord) Hess. John's father George had been a director of the First National Bank of Uniontown.

This family of First Church members lived at 272 West Main Street, which had previously been owned by Mr. and Mrs. C. H. Beall. The Hesses were one of the oldest families west of the Alleghenies, Peter Hess being one of the pioneer settlers of the county.

A "Style Show" at First Presbyterian Church in the 1930s.

Left to Right: Eleanor Mead Stone (modeling her wedding gown), Mrs. Mary Neff White, Henrietta Lowe Rupp, Peggy Campbell Bucher, Blanche Dearth

From the Roaring Twenties through Prohibition, the congregation continued on as people dedicated themselves to the Lord and the ministry of their church. In Uniontown, the American Legion held the first Americanism Day parade in 1934 to combat a communistic plan to stage a May Day parade. In 1937, the WMBS radio station began operating.

When the Japanese bombed Pearl Harbor on December 7, 1941, over 3 million women stood side-by-side with 6 million men on assembly lines as the United States produced war materials and equipment. Around this time, another memorial plaque was dedicated at the Presbyterian Church "in honor of those who represent our church in service of God and country." It contained the names of 89 men and seven women who had served. It is still found on the wall of the church chapel at the time of this writing.

Many of the names found on both memorial plaques can also be spotted throughout the church history archives. Countless other names appear often as well.

MacDonald is one example of a name that frequently dots the pages of the church and Sunday School documents.

Daniel Webster "D. W." MacDonald was the President of the old Baxter Class at First Church for some time, but he was not the first president. Sunday School classes were often named after their original teacher. The Fulton Class and the Spence Bible Class are two of the other classes that met for many years at the church.

D. W.'s son, Herbert S. MacDonald, a former judge of the Supreme Court, once wrote a book entitled *One Small Branch of the Ol' MacDonal' Tree*, a tale of his family's genealogy, which he dedicated to D. W.

Herbert sent a copy of the book to the Baxter Class in February 1969 as a memorial to his father, who had died on November 20, 1931. He hoped it would ultimately "find a resting place in the Sunday School library." At the time of this writing, it is still located on a shelf in the church library. A portion of a tribute to D.W. that was submitted by the Baxter Class can be found on page 90.

Also found on the library shelves are other books authored by church members or friends throughout the years. One writer was a previous First Church minister to whom credit is due for some of the more interesting details of this volume.

Dr. William Blake Hindman arrived at First Church in the fall of 1928. He was a historian who left behind some important notes about the church history. He also authored several booklets about local history to include *Uniting a Nation*, *Drums of Necessity*, and *The National Road*.

During his 1928-1953 pastorate, he became the chairman of the local Fort Necessity Memorial Association. The area where the fort had been located was simply a mass of weeds, and no one could have guessed that a battle which had changed the map of the world had taken place on the site. Dr. Hindman worked for the area to become a National Battlefield site under the care of the National Park Service. In his booklet, *The Great Meadows Campaign and The Climactic Battle of Fort Necessity: Based on newly discovered evidence*, he documents the process and the many prominent figures he had dealings with along the way. Fort Necessity became a National Battlefield in September 1963.

Another historian to appear in the chronicles of the church is elder Judge Edward Dumbauld. Judge Dumbauld was a district judge for the Western District of Pennsylvania. He authored several books about Thomas Jefferson and also one entitled *The Sayings of Jesus, a compilation of the recorded words of Jesus from the New Testament*.

Edward Dumbauld

Notably, Judge Dumbauld was close friends with the Reverand George Macpherson Docherty, who is known as the minister responsible for encouraging President Dwight D. Eisenhower to add the words "under God" to the Pledge of Allegiance.

Rev. Docherty had pastored the New York Avenue Presbyterian Church where Eisenhower attended. It is located two blocks from the White House and has also been attended by President Lincoln and others. During the turmoil of the Cold War, Rev. Docherty's message in his sermon one morning was that any communist country could pledge allegiance to their own flag the same way that Americans pledged to theirs. Yet America had been built on the principle that there is a God, and that the nation has a vertical relationship with Him. Referencing a deity in our Pledge would set the nation apart in both morality and humility. After the sermon, Eisenhower said to the minister, "I think you've got something."

Judge Dumbauld is also remembered by Trinity parishioners for having had a great memory. He is said to have been able to recall many important details of the church history.

Harry Albert, a Trinity church member, said that Judge Dumbauld once agreed to answer questions about the church during a Family Night event.

"Someone asked one question, and it took him 45 minutes to answer it. So, there was no time for any other questions after that. It was just amazing," he said.

When it came to faith, Judge Dumbauld was active in the church and loved to sing to the Lord. John Barnhart, another Trinity Church member, said he remembers a particular time when the congregation was singing a Christmas carol, perhaps Silent Night. "Judge Dumbauld sang it in his native language, German," he said. "We all just sort of softened our voices a little bit and listened. We just let him sing. I remember that service so well."

When the Rev. Dr. John Sharp became pastor of Trinity Church in 1981, he decided that he could not let himself feel intimidated by the astounding intellect of Judge Dumbauld.

He said, chuckling, "One of the interesting things that I can remember is that we were having a congregational meeting for ordinary business. You only did what you announced you were going to do. You didn't bring in other discussion. We were about finished with it, and Judge Dumbauld wanted to make a motion.

According to our rules and order, it was out of order. I had to call the Judge Dumbauld out of order!"

Judge Dumbauld and his wife resided at 44 South Mt. Vernon Avenue, the present location of the WMBS radio station.

A final, memorable author on the selves of Trinity Library is former pastor's wife Charlotte Ross. In May 1980, the church held a reception honoring Charlotte for the publication of her book, *Who is the Minister's Wife?: A Search for Personal Fulfillment.* It promised to answer questions about the minister's wife in modern days and how the changing position of women affected her and her relationship to the church.

Nearly 30 years earlier, on January 28, 1951, the first woman elder of the church had been ordained. Her name was Martha Hankins, and she had been a member since 1918, two years before the 19th Amendment of the Constitution was ratified giving women the right to vote. It was a right known as "women's suffrage." The country continued to see many strides for women's rights since that time, and Mrs. Ross' book surely spoke to many.

In the second half of the twentieth century following World War II, the Presbyterians in Uniontown were not without new challenges, such as the merger of First and Second Presbyterian Churches and the many renovation projects that would ensue. Nevertheless, great victories also graced the two congregations.

The era from 1947-56 is often referred to as "post-war," even though America still faced the Cold War. As the country had eased back into more slightly peaceful times, a prized feature of First Church and then Trinity Church began to develop.

In July 1949, Mr. William T. Rennecker was hired as the first full-time Minister of Music. He was a graduate of Westminster Choir College in Princeton, New Jersey, and had double-majored in organ and voice. He soon created an extensive music program that has been described by Dr. John Sharp as "phenomenal" and "something really to behold."

Believing that music was a mighty factor in human life in its influence on ideas, morals and ideals, Mr. Rennecker once told a Morning Herald journalist that the function of the program was to provide the most effective music possible for the services of Worship, and to be a means of religious and musical education for each chorister.

In the early days of the program, there were five choirs. To begin with, the Cherub Choir was for girls and boys through 7 years of age. They were vested in white robes and collars with large black satin ties. The purpose of having a choir for such young children was said to be for teaching them "basic and real Christian truths as well as the art of reverence." Next, the Junior Choir was for ages 8 through 11, and these youngsters were adorned in maroon robes with white surpluses. Subsequently, the Chapel Choir was for the Secondary School students, and the Choral Union was for adults. Finally, the Men's Chorus was created for men of the church who "enjoyed singing but were too busy to sing in the Union."

Afterwards, several other organists and music directors gave their own talented contributions to the music program. As a result, Trinity Church was long

The Cherub Choir, the Junior Choir, the Chapel Choir, and the Choral Union
1949-50 Season

known for its superb choral realization. In many ways, that is still the case at the time of this writing.

Following the hire of the first music director, First Church members decided to remodel the chancel area of the sanctuary. The Music Committee had long noticed this need and were busy planning for the alterations even before the January session meeting of 1950, when the plans were proposed. Architect and church member T. Ray Fulton presented his drawings, which session decided should also be shown to the congregation for their consideration as well.

The special congregational meeting was held on March 8, 1950, following a Family Night covered dish dinner. Mr. Buell B. Whitehill, chairman of the Music Committee, presented the plan, and Mr. Fulton explained the details. Mr. Renneckar also reported on the poor condition of the organ. The congregation approved a resolution that the changes to the chancel should be made and that a new pipe organ would be installed. The work was to be completed within one year of that very day.

Exactly one year and three days later, the Dedicatory Service was held for the new chancel, with a choir loft that seated 50, and the new 64-rank Austin pipe organ.

Another large project of that decade followed out of necessity. Ever-increasing Sunday School and music program attendance overcrowded the available space at the church. The congregation remodeled the church basement so that there would be ample classroom space. They also modernized the kitchen at the same time. The architect was again T. Ray Fulton of J. C. Fulton & Son.

Around this time, in 1955, the Women's Association was organized. It became a forerunner of the Presbyterian Women, a group that still continues to meet at Trinity Church.

As a result of the many renovation projects, First Church was prepared for the influx of new parishioners when they merged with Second Church in 1962. The new church members brought additional flavor and ideas to Trinity. For instance, the Second Church congregation had long broadcasted their worship services on the WMBS radio station. They brought this tradition with them. At the time of this writing, Trinity Church has continued to broadcast each Sunday morning within a radius of over 100 miles.

In 1965, a new series of additional remodeling projects began. First, a small room just outside of the chancel was reconstructed and furnished to be a Sacris-

The chancel following the 1951 remodel

ty. It is still in use at the time of this writing to store communion ware, to have a place to prepare the elements, and to take care of church chancel flowers. The following year, the basement of Trinity House was upgraded and several rooms of the old manse were painted. Next, in 1970, the church music office, music rooms and pastor's study were redesigned. Finally, church members worked to create, decorate and furnish a "parlor" in 1975.

Finally, the days of great renovations ended, and the later 1980s would usher in extensive repair work. Repairs to the exterior of the structure and especially the rooftops began and have continued even into more recent years.

During the 1970s, banners representing various church creeds were handcrafted by the church women and hung from the arches in the chapel. Each of the eight banners mark important moments in the history of the Christian church when theological statements were adopted, such as the Apostle's Creed. The

The remodeled kitchen in the 1950s

The Nursery Department in the 1950s
Mrs. Paul Totten, teacher

The Primary Department in the 1950s
Miss Edith Selong, teacher

The Kindergarten Group in the 1950s
Miss Jean Arnett and Mrs. Nancy Tudor, teachers

The Junior Department in the 1950s
Mrs. James Hazen and Mrs. E. T. Porter Jr., teachers

Chronicle of a Legacy

Mrs. Albert A. Coffman, 1979
(Mary Martha Lorenzo)

creeds span 1,600 years starting with the fourth century and ending with the twentieth.

The banners, like Trinity Church itself, show that even as time brings with it many changes, some concepts remain the same, namely faith. Mary Martha Lorenzo, for one, holds onto hope that Trinity Church and the current building will both remain for many years to come. Mary Martha is a Trinity Church member and a former church secretary. She retired from her position in 1985.

"I think it will always be there. There will always be a Trinity," she said, matter-of-factly. And then, "As far as I'm concerned, there will be. I hope so. It will go on."

Mary Martha and others have great hopes for the old structure of Trinity Church, but the future cannot be known.

Dr. Sharp offered that unless there is a major shift in the Uniontown population, Trinity will not have a robust congregation to properly care for the large edifice. As a result, many of the priceless heirlooms contained in the building will be at risk.

"So much of it is irreplaceable," he said. "So, you're always kind of caught in a vice about it, because the faith we know is not in a building."

Dr. Sharp said that the church members justify maintaining the aging building because the artistic beauty is evidence of a bygone era.

"The faith that was expressed in those ages was a triumphant one," he said. "The hymns have a marching sound to them."

When it comes to the future of the building, Dr. Sharp gave the following wisdom: "We are in a time now when we are looking more for a personal faith that relates people to people. However, I think we need to be aware that it took a lot of dedication and interest to put such expression into Trinity. You have to marvel at their ability to have put it together. But we have to also be keen to the fact that faith does not always lead us to build temples."

Although the tales in this volume have recorded the names of some who contributed greatly to Trinity Church through the years, this writer could have never hoped to record them all. A myriad of stories have been lived out with Trinity Church as a backdrop.

Be that as it may, we can be certain of one fact. Untold names are also woven into the very fabric of the church. They are found on plaques in various locations, on hymnal covers, Bibles, books, and even on the bell tower walls. They are listed on page upon page in the many registers and minute books. They are on letters, on Sunday School attendance charts, and on backs of photographs - all in dusty, preservation boxes. Some are too faded now to read, and some were never physically recorded at all.

However, even those whose names are not remembered are still felt in the spirit of the place, for they have left behind portions of their hearts. Their memories cling to the church and will follow it even beyond the building, wherever the fellowship may go. From the potluck dinners, to the Christmas Eve candlelight services, to the private prayers whispered in the sanctuary. Fun stories, such as a bat dropping to the feet of the shocked choir, or a frantic rush to cut food into smaller portions in order to serve an unexpected increase in dinner guests. Love and laughter echo on.

Although only a breath of a summary of the many recollections are documented here, it is the hope of this writer that we reflect on what was left out. All those who have ever brushed Trinity Church have given of themselves to its life, for better or worse, just the same.

For this, we remember them.

Sources

Newspapers:

Zajac, Francis Borsodi. "Historic Oak Grove Cemetery Offers Link to Past." *The Herald-Standard* [Uniontown] 27 Nov. 2011: n.p. *heraldstandard.com*. Web. 19 Nov. 2015.

"Corner Stone Laid.: Ceremony at the New Presbyterian Church." *The News Standard* [Uniontown] 18 June 1894: 1. Print.

"Extensive Program of Music at First Presbyterian Church." *The Morning Herald* [Uniontown] 12 Sept. 1950: 11. Print.

Gibb, Tom. "How the Pledge got God." *Pittsburgh Post-Gazette* 28 June 2002: n.p. *post-gazette.com*. Web. 19 Nov. 2015.

Webpages:

Owens, Al. "Did You Know? - XCIII" *Al Owens In Print*. Al Owens, Jan. 2010. Web. 10 Nov. 2015. <http://www.thinkwebworks.com/AO/History.asp?ID=132> "36. The Gilded Age." *U.S. History*. U.S. History, n.d. Web. 13 Nov. 2015. <http://www.history.org/us/36.asp>

Book:

Semans, Pauline R. *Beesontown: A Look Into the Past*. New York: Carlton Press, Inc., 1978. Print.

Church Records:

History of Redstone. Washington: Observer Book and Job Print, 1889. Print.

Hindman, William B. *Brief History of the First Presbyterian Church Uniontown Pa*. Uniontown, n.d. Print
(Notes left behind by the Rev. Dr. William Blake Hindman) First Presbyterian Church Register and Minute Book, 1825 - 1851

Keller, David F. *When Asbury Church Was Built 75 Years Ago*. Uniontown; 1995. Print.
(Church Pamphlet)

First Presbyterian Church Register

Personal Interviews

pastors

William T. Wylie | 1819-1823

J. H. Agnew | 1828-1831

Joel Stoneroad | 1831-1842

Andrew Ferrier, D.D. | 1842-1844

Griffith Owen | 1845-1847

Moses Allen Williams | 1849-1852

James H. Callen | 1853-1855

William H. Hamilton | 1856-1866

Walter W. Ralston | 1867-1873

Samuel S. Gilson | 1874-1879

First Presbyterian Church

A. S. Milholland, D.D. | 1880-1905

W. Hamilton Spence, Litt. D., D.D. | 1906-1923

William R. Van Buskirk, D.D. | 1923-1927

William Blake Hindman, L.L.D., D.D. | 1928-1953

William R. Johnston, D.D. | 1954-1961

Second Presbyterian Church

Seth R. Gordon, D.D. | 1894-1906

W. Scott Bowman, D.D. | 1907-1924

A. H. Hibshman, Ph.D. | 1924-1929

James C. Clark, D.D. | 1929-1946

John V. Berger, D.D. | 1947-1958

Wilbur F. Christy | 1959-1962

Trinity United Presbyterian Church

Vincent T. Ross, D.D. | 1962-1980

John K. Sharp, D.Min. | 1981-2000

Michael I. Orsted | 2003-2013

James W. Gear M.Div. | 2016-present

about the author

Meg Grimm is the secretary at Trinity United Presbyterian Church. She has a love for history, folklore and old church buildings. Meg lives in Ohiopyle, Pennsylvania with her husband Max and dog Bill. Her other books can be found at StorySpinnerBooks.com.

For more about Meg Grimm, visit StorySpinnerBooks.com

Visit Trinity United Presbyterian Church online:

www.trinityupc.com

www.ingramcontent.com/pod-product-compliance
Lightning Source LLC
LaVergne TN
LVHW091551060526
838200LV00036B/788